Christmas Past

Christmas Past

Gavin Weightman
& Steve Humphries

SIDGWICK & JACKSON
LONDON

First published in Great Britain in 1987
by Sidgwick & Jackson Limited

Copyright © 1987 by London Weekend Television

Designed by Michael Head

ISBN 0-283-99531-9

Photoset by Rowland Phototypesetting Limited
Bury St Edmunds, Suffolk
Printed in Great Britain by
Butler & Tanner Limited, Frome and London
for Sidgwick & Jackson Limited
1 Tavistock Chambers, Bloomsbury Way
London WC1A 2SG

Contents

Picture Acknowledgements

The picture on page 106 is reproduced by gracious permission of Her Majesty the Queen. All other photographs and illustrations were supplied or are reproduced by kind permission of the following: BBC Hulton Picture Library, 82, 94, 102/3, 118/9, 122/3, 154/5, 167 (top); Beamish North of England Open Air Museum, 77 (bottom), 146, 158; Terry Borton, 139; Bridgeman Art Library, 78/9; British Library, 144; Mrs Cartwright, 51; Christmas Archive, 13, 22/3, 46, 74/5, 105; Church Army Archives, 14, 58/9; Colindale, 11, 25, 28, 42, 48, 52, 62, 89, 92, 108, 113, 114/5, 128, 130/1, 135, 141, 142, 162 (inset); Documentary Photography Archive, 38/9, 133; Howarth-Loomes Collection, 110; Henry Kinaird, 19; John Kitchen, 167 (bottom); Doug Lear, 65, 152/3; Mansell Collection 9, 14/15, 20; The Photo Source, 44/5, 100 (top), 161, 169; Popperfoto, 36, 98/9, 100 (bottom), 148; The Salvation Army, 70; Topham, 54/5, 72 (bottom), 86/7, 120, 125, 127, 136/7, 149, 150/1, 162/3, 170, 173; Ullstein Bilderdienst, 26; Victoria and Albert Museum, 32, 33, 34.

Introduction

INTRODUCTION

Christmas Past is not, as the title might imply, a nostalgic look at the great feasts of our ancestors, the quaint customs of rural England, nor a dreary resurrection of Dickensian family jollity. This book, and the London Weekend Television programme it accompanies, is about the way in which the Christmas rituals that are familiar to everyone today – the stockings, and cards, and crackers – became a 'tradition' in our society, and the reasons why they have become such important rites for people to perform each year.

There is a widely held view that Christmas has lost its former meaning, that it has been spoiled by 'commercialization', and that it is nothing more than a giant confidence trick imposed on a reluctant nation by advertisers and the manufacturers of seasonal gifts. In many people there is an uneasiness about the compulsion they feel to celebrate it – to perform the seasonal ritual – and a deep suspicion of the welter of imagery on television and in shops, from the artificial snow to the old gentleman clad in red robes.

Christmas does demand a kind of conformity to social rules which can either be oppressive or very pleasing, according to your stage in life and your general feelings about acquiescing to social pressure. It is a very strange season for an industrial, and supposedly rational society – for it engenders a kind of collective will to fantasize; to pretend it is snowing when clearly it is not; to embrace family ties when relations are strained; to be nice to people who at other times of the year you cannot stand; to make believe that Santa Claus is coming, and go to great lengths to convince young children that he has been and gone, leaving presents behind him.

Everybody knows how the Christmas ritual *ought* to be performed: if you have, say, spaghetti bolognese or curry for Christmas lunch something has gone very wrong. Yet historically, this feeling that there is a 'proper' way to observe Christmas is quite recent. This is not simply the result of the twentieth-century commercial pressure to conformity. The modern Christmas ritual – the one that we recognize today – arose and took shape in that era of our history during which,

Previous pages: A classic scene from the Victorian family Christmas at the time it was emerging as the most popular festival in Britain

Opposite: Father Christmas in his new guise as Santa Claus, bringer of gifts for children. He arrived from America in the 1870s

"HERE WE ARE AGAIN!!"

in many respects, a patchwork of local and regional cultures was transformed into a national culture in which people came to act and think in much the same way, much of the time.

At the beginning of Queen Victoria's reign, in 1837, no British children hung their stockings by a fireplace on Christmas Eve; nobody had heard of Santa Claus; Christmas crackers did not exist; very few people ate turkey on Christmas Day; it was not common to give presents; and the decorated and lighted Christmas tree was hardly known outside the Royal Court. In fact, in 1837 – and for a long time afterwards amongst a large section of the British people – Christmas Day was not a very important date in the calendar for feasting or any kind of social ritual. It was not observed as a holiday in many regions. There were winter feast days, and special occasions on which many Christmas-like rituals were observed, but they took place sporadically and locally between All Hallows Day on 1 November and Candlemas on 2 February. In the newspapers and magazines of the early nineteenth century little mention is made of Christmas Day. It was between the 1830s and the 1930s that the modern Christmas ritual began to take shape in one section of society – principally the middle classes. Christmas acquired new customs, became more or less fixed as a celebration which took place on 25 December, and spread like a fashion through the regions and social classes of Britain. In this sense, *Christmas Past* is not so much about the survival of tradition in contemporary society, as a tradition created by that society.

At first this is a difficult point to grasp, because most of the imagery of Christmas today seems to us to be old-fashioned: the stage coaches, the skating on frozen ponds, the figure of Santa coming down a chimney long after the arrival of central heating and the passing of the Clean Air Act of 1956 left many homes without open fires. In some ways the Christmas celebration is out of date now, for it was formed at the beginnings of modern society in the nineteenth century, and is set in an aspic of Victorian sentimentality. Yet the Christmas ritual is modern, in so far as it reflects a host of social and economic changes that transformed society in the nineteenth century, and which are still working themselves out today.

In piecing together the social change and technological strands which created the modern Christmas, we discover a great deal about the intimate lives of British people. The story of Christmas becomes a vivid account of how culturally divided the nation was, and how in the

Though we think of him as a 'traditional' figure, Santa Claus – pictured here as an American nineteenth-century Christmas card – was a creation of the modern era

13

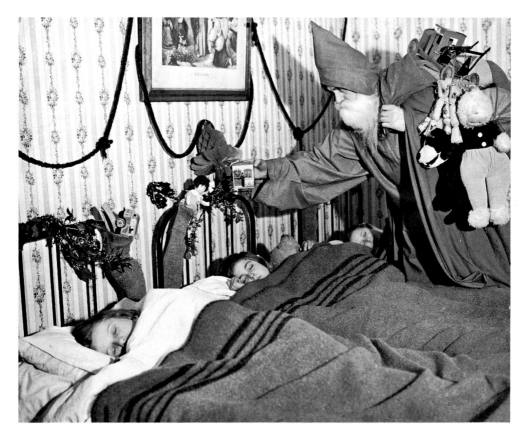

Father Christmas visits a Church Army Motherless Children's Home in 1935

age of affluence and mass communications a kind of conformity came about – superficial though it may still be.

So this book is not just about the creation of the single most important national festival in Britain. It is also about the way in which the everyday lives of people have changed; for the celebration of Christmas touches on just about every aspect of social experience – families, work, wealth, leisure, entertainment and, perhaps most significantly, the relationship between the haves and the have-nots in society.

It is this last point – the way in which the celebration of Christmas throws into sharp relief the social and regional divisions in Britain over the last century and a half – which is the central focus of *Christmas Past*. This is not an arbitrary emphasis, for Christmas – or at least the period of winter revelry which has existed for centuries and pre-dates the Christian Nativity – has always been a time in which social differences are, for a brief period, forgotten or levelled out. Normal, workaday values are overturned; everything is 'topsy-turvy'; the rich lie down with the poor. The attempts to close the social divide at Christmas serve to emphasize how great the gulf is in normal times – an aspect of the festival which was not lost on Charles Dickens, the great reformer and the conscience of the Victorian middle classes, who tried to harness the festival to his own philanthropic intentions and in doing so helped to re-invent the 'Spirit of Christmas'.

The Christmas ritual which we know today was the 'invention' of the relatively well-to-do Victorian middle classes, and reflects their preoccupations: a deep-seated fear of the rift between rich and poor in the cauldron of industrialism; a worship of family as opposed to communal ties; a new interest in protecting children from the harshness of the real world; and a nostalgic view of how life used to be in 'Merrie Olde Englande' before the satanic mills of manufacture destroyed the mythical past of rural harmony. Victorian reformers and doe-eyed do-gooders were only too well aware that the mass of the population could not celebrate Christmas as they did, and first promoted the festival by charitable endeavours. In workhouses and prisons inmates were entertained to an institutionalized form of the family ritual long before the deserving and undeserving poor could expect a Christmas tree, a turkey, or a bulging stocking on Christmas morning. It was charity that enabled the poor to celebrate Christmas, and for a very long time one of the most poignant emotions for a comfortable family was the knowledge that they had made a pauper happy at Christmas.

In time, this charitable aspect of Christmas faded in significance (though it still exists), and the promotion of the festival was taken up by the various forms of mass communications and commercial interests. All these held up one way, and one way only, of celebrating a proper Christmas; that was the middle-class Christmas. But it took a long time for the mass of the people to have the wherewithall to join in the celebrations without the help of a charitable hand-out. The story of *Christmas Past* is an account of the development of a ritual which may seem to us today to be quaint and irrational, but is in fact in all its garish and baubled glory, a glittering and sentimental account of the way our social world has changed since Scrooge bowed to the Christmas Spirit, and was humbled by the Humbug of the Season.

The Christmas Empire

CHAPTER ONE

Any visitor to the remote farming communities of Perthshire in Scotland on 25 December 1919 would hardly have noticed that this was Christmas Day. Henry Kinaird was a schoolboy then. Though he and his friends hung their stockings on Christmas Eve and on the next day found in them an orange and a bit of fruit, life went on more or less as normal:

> We didn't have a holiday on Christmas Day, we went to school. It felt quite normal because work was going on in the farms and in the villages; shops were working, and, aye, the mills were working. There was a soup kitchen which was run during the winter for six months, and as a special treat for Christmas the soup was made with a chicken or boiling fowl, and you got pieces of chicken in the soup, which went down well, of course.

At about the same time, thousands of miles from England, in Poona, India, Marie Lenihan was enjoying the elaborate Christmas rituals of British expatriates:

> On Christmas afternoon we went with Miriam, our ayah [nurse], to the Gymkhana Club to meet Father Christmas. We knew he was coming because we'd hear the tom-tom, the cymbals, and the general pandemonium. And then he was led in by the attendant on an elephant. The elephant had its toe-nails painted and its tusks and its eyes were marked out, and it had a green, scarlet, and gold cloth on its back, and Father Christmas. We all broke ranks and rushed towards him, and he walked on to the stage with his sacks, called our names and gave us presents.

On the face of it, it is quite extraordinary that the modern Christmas ritual should have been more fully acknowledged and celebrated by the British Raj in India than by communities shivering back home in a genuine British winter. But the modern Christmas festival was not adopted by the population *en masse* in a sudden burst of enthusiasm. For a number of reasons, the new ritual spread slowly through the

Previous pages: The British Raj improvise a traditional Christmas in India in the 1880s

Henry Kinaird, who as a boy in rural Scotland remembers going to school on Christmas Day

regions and social classes of Britain, reaching Scotland in its full form last of all. The single most important check to its adoption by the mass of people was poverty – they simply could not afford to celebrate like the well-to-do. But there were other factors as well, for Christmas had a different *meaning* as it developed for different sections of the population.

For the expatriates in India, celebrating Christmas was a reminder of home, a re-affirmation of Englishness, and a gesture of national and international loyalty and unity. For the Scots, however, Christmas was essentially an English festival which they resisted, partly for their own nationalistic reasons, and partly because of a fundamental difference in religious beliefs. The Presbyterian Church had set itself against the festival because they believed it essentially pagan with no authority in the New Testament. This same objection had been voiced in the seventeenth century by the English Puritans, and lingered on in nonconformist areas of the north of England until the early nineteenth century. Scotland and other northern regions had their own, rival, celebrations held at New Year or Hogmanay.

It was the kind of Christmas celebration which expatriates took with them to India that was to become the nationally accepted form of winter festival. The Scottish adherence to Hogmanay is really a survival of an older 'regionalism' which was swept away by the forces which spread the new Christmas rituals in the nineteenth and twentieth centuries.

A host of customs, with many local variations, predated the modern festival and differed from it in quite marked ways. There was, in effect, a long winter season of feast days lasting from the beginning of November until the end of January, with Christmas Day only one date in the calendar and not necessarily the most important in village celebrations. In rural communities, as in the cider-producing areas of the West Country, the highlight of the season might be the wassailing of apple trees. This took place usually in the first week in January, and was essentially a kind of pagan fertility rite to keep away bad spirits and to encourage the trees to bear fruit. Like many such customs it took place out of doors, and involved a great deal of drinking and revelry. In other places, Plough Monday (when agricultural workers toured a village extracting some kind of gift in money or kind from the wealthier households) would be the most important winter event. This, too, usually took place in January, as did many of the bonfire ceremonies which were related to pagan sunworship rather than Christianity.

Until quite late in the nineteenth century, there was really no nationally agreed way of celebrating around Christmastime. In the north, New Year remained a more important day for revelry, and in all regions and amongst all social classes Twelfth Night was still observed as a significant event. This was when special cakes were baked and other rituals performed (see Chapters Two and Six).

As the Victorian middle-class Christmas developed, it concentrated the festival into two days – Christmas Day and Boxing Day. It was essentially a domestic, family festival, as opposed to a village event, and brought its feasting and merrymaking indoors. As it became more popular, the customs of rural England died out: they were inappropriate in the towns which grew rapidly in the nineteenth century. Other feast days, in particular Twelfth Night (6 January), lost their importance as the newly popular way of celebrating absorbed and adapted the customs associated with them and made them part of the traditional family Christmas ritual. For example, the Christmas cake was borrowed from Twelfth Night celebrations, and the Christmas

The traditional Christmas, complete with plum pudding, reached the remotest parts of the Empire before it was a common celebration among Britain's poor

cracker provided a miniature and refined version of customs in which fires were lit and people dressed up in strange clothes and funny hats (see Chapter Two).

In effect, the Victorian pioneers of the modern Christmas rolled the old feast days into one short, respectable family event. The transformation began around the 1830s – the cracker was invented in 1840 – and was more or less complete by the 1870s, which was when the familiar figure of Santa Claus first appeared in Britain. However, though the new ritual was fully formed, it was by no means a *national* festival, for many regions still held on to older customs, and the accepted way of celebrating was well beyond the means of the mass of the population.

St Distaff's Day – the day after Twelfth Night – in the early nineteenth century. This type of midwinter revelry died out as the Victorians promoted the 'family Christmas'

The disappearance of older rituals, and the adoption by the mass of the population of the modern festival, has been the result of a constellation of forces and influences: the desire of the middle classes to spread their own values to the poorer sections of society; the rise of new means to create a national culture; the breakdown of regionalism; and, of course, the exploitation of the festival by commercial interests.

The Victorian middle classes were not content simply to enjoy in the privacy of their own homes this remodelled Christmas festival. The contrast between their way of celebrating, with turkeys, lighted trees, presents around a blazing fire, and the miserable conditions of the poor at Christmas touched their conscience.

Quite quickly, bringing Christmas to the poor took on the characteristics of a kind of moral crusade. On the one hand it assuaged the guilt of the well-to-do; on the other there was the hope that the rougher elements of society might abandon their raucous communal

festivities and adopt the calmer, less threatening behaviour of the middle classes. As they extolled the virtues of the traditional family Christmas – and through charitable endeavour took it to the poor in their homes, in the workhouses, and in prisons – the well-to-do began to turn the festival into a celebration of national unity; a decorative covering for the deep divisions that existed in society.

It was during the nineteenth century that the creation of a national culture first became possible and began to break down regional differences such as local customs and language. The development of the railways was an important influence, as was the introduction of state education later in the century, and the rise of popular newspapers. The emerging national culture adopted and invented 'traditions' to express social unity. It was in this period, from Queen Victoria's Diamond Jubilee in 1897, that the English gift for royal pageantry developed. The rise and spread of the 'traditional' Christmas played a part in the creation of this new kind of national culture. Characteristically, it took on a folksy imagery of past glory that harked back to a mythical 'Merrie Olde Englande', full of beaming squires and merry peasants frolicking together in grand halls.

Christmas became bound up with nationalism, and later in the nineteenth century with Imperialism. In the 1880s, Christmas trees were often decked out with Union Jacks and the flags of the Empire; toy soldiers of British regiments reached a peak of popularity in the late nineteenth century; and people made plum puddings with Empire ingredients.

Much of the imagery and the ritual of the new festival came from Britain's great international rival, Germany. Most toys were made there, the decorated and lighted tree was German, and many of the early Christmas cards were printed there.

In Germany, Christmas celebrations had become important in national unity. This association of a particular way of celebrating Christmas with nationalism produced a quite bizarre and very moving episode on the Western Front in 1914. As Christmas approached there was no official truce or cease-fire called by the warring governments, and there appears to have been no expectation that any concession would be made to the season. But the Christmas festival had gained a powerful hold on the hearts and minds of the ordinary men on both sides. British tommies had gathered bits of holly to decorate dug-outs, but their officers appeared to have made no special arrangements for Christmas Day. The Germans, however, were much better served.

The Union Jack, rather than a fairy, tops the tree of a well-to-do family as Christmas becomes a celebration of national unity

THE ILLUSTRATED LONDON NEWS

CHRISTMAS NUMBER

DECEMBER 1876

Nos. 1951, 1952.

VOL. LXIX.

HOISTING THE UNION JACK. BY ALFRED HUNT.

Christmas trees (many of them small enough for dug-outs), as well as food hampers, were issued to the men at the Front. There was no doubt this was to boost morale and keep up their nationalistic spirit. However, these efforts backfired, and on Christmas Eve – the high point of the festival for the Germans – the British tommies were confronted by an extraordinary sight. It so moved them that instead of fighting more enthusiastically for King and country they laid down their arms to embrace the enemy. Graham Williams was there on that remarkable night:

> My turn of duty on the sentry was from ten to twelve. I was standing there, gazing out, and I thought what a different Christmas this was going to be from any I'd ever had before. I thought that my family back home would be putting up their decorations as they always did after supper on Christmas Eve, and my father would be thinking about making his rum punch. I looked at my watch and at eleven I was standing there – it was exactly midnight by German time – and I suddenly saw lights appear in front of me all along the German trenches. I was wondering what was happening, and they started singing *Stille Nacht* – Silent Night. I'd not heard it before and I thought what a beautiful tune it was.

It was the start of an unofficial truce on the Western Front, which lasted up to six weeks in many places, with British and German soldiers exchanging cigarettes and food, and showing each other pictures of their families. It did not meet with official approval, and opposing soldiers who had embraced each other were moved off so the battle could recommence. In later Christmases, the British Army made sure that it provided a proper festival for its own men, and encouraged them to regard it not in terms of 'goodwill to all men' but as a form of loyalty to the British flag.

By the end of the Great War, Christmas was clearly becoming *the* popular winter celebration throughout most of Britain. Even then, however, the Scots were resisting the spread of this English festival. Janet MacCormick, whose father was a shipyard worker in Glasgow, experienced as a child a peculiar Scottish mix of old tradition and new Christmas customs – the hanging of stockings: 'My father was very strict Presbyterian and New Year was the only time you could hang your stocking, Christmas was a time to sing carols and go to church. No Christmas dinner, no Christmas pudding; it was like every other day of the week.'

The unofficial truce on the Western front proved the remarkable power of the new Christmas festival

THE ILLUSTRATED LONDON NEWS.

REGISTERED AS A NEWSPAPER FOR TRANSMISSION IN THE UNITED KINGDOM, AND TO CANADA AND NEWFOUNDLAND BY MAGAZINE POST.

No 3951. · VOL. CXLVI.   SATURDAY, JANUARY 9, 1915.   SIXPENCE.

The Copyright of all the Editorial Matter, both Engravings, and Letterpress, is Strictly Reserved in Great Britain, the Colonies, Europe, and the United States of America.

Though Charles McEwan's schoolfriends celebrated Christmas, his country grandmother would not hear of it, even though the family lived in Edinburgh:

> Most of the presents in our family were given by Gran, because we were quite poor, and she would always give them on New Year's morning. They'd be wrapped in brown paper – no decorative paper in those days. I once, in all innocence, asked her: 'Why do we not celebrate Christmas? Why is it the New Year?' Her answer still staggers me; she said: 'We're no heathens, laddie.' I think what she meant was that the English celebrated Christmas and they were heathens.

The conversion of the Scots to Christmas was the result of a great build-up of social pressure, which became more and more powerful in the twentieth century. Janet MacCormick can remember when her father bowed to English custom: 'When I was about six years old Christmas morning there was a knock at the door, and there were three of my little friends with Christmas presents. We looked at my mother and said: "Why can't we hang our stockings at Christmas?" Father Christmas had passed our chimney; we were devastated. My mother spoke to my father, and that was the last time we missed Christmas.'

Whereas in the nineteenth century it was the charitable zeal of the middle classes which had chiefly been responsible for popularizing the new festival, in the twentieth century more effective means arose to encourage conformity to Christmas rituals. There were many more popular magazines and newspapers, the cinemas, and then radio. In many aspects of social life, the BBC was influential in creating a national culture, and it became important not only in the popularization of Christmas but in establishing its 'meaning'.

A landmark in this use of Christmas as a celebration, not only of the home and family but of national and Imperial togetherness, came with the first ever Royal Christmas message, broadcast by King George V from Sandringham House in 1932. It was not the King's idea, but the inspiration of John (later Lord) Reith, the General Manager of the British Broadcasting Company. In 1923, before the company, the forerunner of the British Broadcasting Corporation, had got its Royal charter, John Reith had approached the King with a request for him to give a Christmas or New Year message to the nation. He argued that

It was the ordinary German soldiers, issued with Christmas trees by the army, who initiated the 1914 truce

such a gesture would make a 'national moral impression' and help to boost the sales of radio manufacturers who were struggling at the time. The King turned him down. In 1932, when his company had its Royal Charter and had become the BBC as we know it today, Reith tried again. It was just a few months after the BBC had inaugurated its Empire Service, and this time the King agreed.

The time of the broadcast, 3 p.m., was chosen to achieve maximum coverage on the Imperial airwaves – though it has remained rather inconvenient to people eating their Christmas dinners in Britain. In his 1934 message, King George described Christmas as 'the festival of the family' and made play about the peoples of the Empire being bound together as 'one big family'. For the British colonialists who had taken the festival to India, Malaysia, China, and the four corners of the world, the King's message provided a direct tie with the home for which they longed.

The way Christmas was spent in the colonies became a popular topic in magazines like *The Lady*. Here is one account of Christmas in Singapore in 1923:

> At Christmas-time, the ex-patriated Englishman, cheered by the memory of Christmases at 'home' throws off his despondency and makes the most of the occasion.
>
> Stringy tasteless roast beef is served as a matter of sentiment and the exile smiles approval when the native cook brings in a stodgy plum-pudding decorated with the orthodox sprig of holly – especially imported from some Indian hill station.

From the same magazine in 1936 there is a very touching account of a Christmas in Kenya, which expresses nicely the importance and meaning of Christmas for the colonial in this period:

> Everyone helped to decorate the Christmas Tree with candles, bright baubles sent from a sixpenny store in London and presents for everyone. The tree was set on the lawn and children romped around it till 6 p.m. . . . As I stood on the verandah watching my guests for a moment it seemed to me we had created a strange scene, a patch of gay, civilized English life in the heart of a wilderness that is as vast as the sea. Even as I watched I heard the crashing roar of a lion . . .

While this little bit of England was being re-created in Africa, a large part of the population back home was still celebrating Christmas in a much less elaborate way. Between the wars, the British Christmas tree was rare in the homes of ordinary people. In London, poor people still took their Christmas dinner – which would certainly not be turkey, but might be a piece of beef – to be cooked in a baker's oven. Chicken was a luxury. In their stockings children still got an apple, an orange, a new penny, and maybe some sweets.

Madge Strachan was brought up in a poor part of Glasgow. In her district there was a will to celebrate Christmas, but no possibility of it being anything like the classic Dickensian family affair:

> We lived in a room and kitchen and we ran into the kitchen and all the stockings were hanging on the mantelpiece and they would be stuffed three-quarters full with newspapers. We got a beautiful orange, a new penny, a piece of shortbread, and a toffee. Then you went down to play with your pals to see what they got, and nearly everybody got the same thing. You had your broth first, a big beautiful pot of broth, then we went down to a bit of spare ground they called the garden and a man came in, lit a big bonfire, and we roasted our tatties in that and all the black came on your face, and we sang carols, chapping our wee hands to keep warm.

This was the reality of Christmas for a great many children between the wars; their only chance of a proper Christmas dinner was at some charity function or other. These charity functions – dinners provided for hundreds of children by the mayor or the local police – were a popular topic with the cinema newsreels around Christmas. At the same time, the newsreels would show sentimental pictures of family Christmases, with mum stirring the Christmas pudding in suburbia, and dad putting up the decorations. These images, and the message that came from radio, in a sense popularized the middle-class festival long before it was a possibility for the majority.

However, from quite early on in the development of the festival there were commercial interests which sought to exploit it, and in so doing helped to popularize Christmas. This really only became poss-ible on a large scale once the festival had become widely accepted, providing a ready-made market. In this respect, the history of Christ-mas cards is interesting, for they were unknown in the first forty years of the nineteenth century, and it was not common to send them until the 1870s.

The invention of the Christmas card is generally attributed to Henry Cole who, in 1843, had a thousand printed to sell in his London art shop. They cost one shilling, which was a very high price. At first, they were not much of a success, for there was no established ritual of sending greetings cards at Christmas. In that period, annual greetings

"Yearly will I do this rite."

A HAPPY NEW YEAR.

A MERRY CHRISTMAS.

Some early Christmas cards from the 1880s, illustrating the confusion of imagery which arose when the tradition of sending greetings shifted from New Year to Christmas

We come to greet thee with A Merry Christmas!

"From farthest shore they come at merry pace,
Swift as the wind, Old Christmas time to grace."

GLAD BE THY CHRISTMAS. HAPPY THY NEW YEAR!

The pagan themes on Christmas cards survived until 'traditional' Christmas imagery evolved in the late nineteenth century

were exchanged at the New Year. A number of other attempts were made to interest the public in cards at Christmastime, but they failed. It seems that the possibility of commercial exploitation and mass production of cards had to wait until the 1870s when the Christmas festival had finally become fully established and had overshadowed rival feast days such as New Year and Twelfth Night. The development of cheaper post helped as well.

In this transition period, when the time for greetings was shifting from New Year to Christmas, there seems to have been a confusion about the themes appropriate for the new cards. New Year was never a religious festival, whereas Christmas was clearly Christian. Yet many of the early card designs were frankly pagan – naked nymphs were popular – or quite irrelevant to the season. As the greeting card industry gathered momentum it began to develop a more 'Christmasy' flavour and, in turn, promoted the now traditional imagery of Christmas.

This had begun in the late nineteenth century. In 1883, *The Times* reported:

It has created quite a new trade, and has opened up a new field of labour for artists, lithographers, engravers, printers, ink and pasteboard makers. . . . All the year round brains are at work devising new designs and inventing novelties. The very cheap

34

Christmas cards come from Germany where they can be produced at a much cheaper rate, but all the more artistic and more highly finished cards are the result of English workmanship.

Many of the early Christmas cards were works of art and sold for up to five guineas. Between the wars, however, mass production brought the price – and standards of illustration – down to the point where millions of people could afford to send them. By this time one of the most popular images was that of Father Christmas, or Santa Claus, and his arrival in the 1870s had also been very significant in the popularizing and commercialization of the Christmas festival. The giving of presents as well as the sending of greetings was still done at New Year rather than Christmas until the last quarter of the nineteenth century. However, the new rituals associated with Santa Claus (see Chapter Seven) shifted present giving to Christmas, and greatly increased the festival's potential for commercial interests.

Between the wars, the beginnings of a mass Christmas market were quite evident, with down-market department stores like Woolworths selling enormous quantities of cheap gifts in December. This was the only time of year most children could expect any sort of present, and three-quarters of all toys were sold at Christmas. There were complaints even then that it had already become a festival perpetuated by commercial interest for its own profit and that it had lost its meaning. But Christmas was still developing as a national festival and had not yet achieved the significance it was to enjoy in the post-war years.

The outbreak of the Second World War in many ways helped to spread enthusiasm for Christmas as a national festival. In this war – in contrast to the first year of the Great War – every effort was made to see that the troops, both British and American, had a good Christmas. For many this meant a better Christmas dinner than they could have expected back home. For some Scotsmen, who barely knew how Christmas should be celebrated, this was a time of conversion to the new festival. Charles McEwan, whose grandmother had banned Christmas at home in Edinburgh when he was a child, found the festival in Italy:

When I was regraded after Anzio, I went back to Rome and Allied Command and we were really in with a lot of English blokes, and we found out that they were an awfully nice bunch. When it came to Christmastime they used to say: 'Leave it to us, Jock!' and they would provide food, bake, and do all sorts. That was the time we really discovered Christmas and carried on this tradition of thinking so much about it. It was great – my granny was wrong!

Charles McEwan, and his wife Betty – who also discovered Christmas during the war – began to celebrate Christmas in earnest when they had young children. They did so in an era of growing post-war affluence, when real wages rose fast, and they were soon buying Christmas trees, and enormous presents for each other – such as a washing machine.

For the great majority in Britain, the full celebration of the family Christmas with all the trimmings only became a possibility in the consumer society of the late 1950s. It was then that all public services – such as the trains and the post – began to close down at Christmas as everyone expected to be able to spend it with their families. Christmas Day was finally made a public holiday in Scotland in 1958.

From the mid 1950s, television provided the last and easily the most powerful means for turning the celebration of Christmas into a truly national event. Half or more of the entire population would watch the same Christmas Day programmes which included from 1957 onwards the Royal message, still broadcast at 3 p.m. By drawing people into the home, and making the celebration more and more a domestic event for the majority, television was a means for achieving the Victorian ideal of the family gathering – though it was not necessarily the kind of occasion the moralists of an earlier era would have wanted. The arrival of television with advertising from the mid 1950s also greatly increased the power of commercial interests to exploit the festival. The Christmas first promoted by the Victorian middle classes, and carrying with it as it developed many of their concerns and values, had in the years of post-war affluence become a kind of social and economic 'empire' which had swamped and eliminated many local and regional customs. In doing so, it had subtlely altered the meaning of the festival for the nation and achieved considerable success in turning a season of misrule into one of morality, as we see in the next chapter.

The classic family Christmas did not become a reality for the mass of the population until after the Second World War

Misrule and Morality

CHAPTER TWO

There is in the Christmas Spirit a most peculiar and uneasy confusion of impulses and sentiments. In the singing of carols and the coming together of families, there is a kind of sugary piety which affects the mass of people who do not go to church or pay much attention to their kith and kin at other times of the year. At the same time, there is a sense that this is a time for revelry, drinking, and eating too much, and generally breaking the rules of humdrum, workaday life.

This tension between misrule and morality is not peculiar to the modern Christmas, nor is it essentially a creation of the Victorians. It arises from the origins of the Christmas festival itself. Puritans were never happy about the excesses of the Christmas season, and what people get up to in the name of the Nativity has embarrassed the Christian Church for a very long time. But, as with other aspects of the festival, the Victorian middle classes did radically change the balance between paganism and piety in Christmas celebrations. In remodelling it they sought – sometimes deliberately and sometimes unconsciously – to retain the jollity and licence of older customs but to keep them under control. And, in effect, they more or less succeeded in domesticating those Saturnalian impulses of the season.

This taming of the spirit of misrule was quite remarkable, for there was absolutely nothing in the new rituals adopted by the Victorians – the tree, present giving, Santa Claus, and so on – that has any Christian meaning at all. In the New Testament there is no reference to Christmas customs nor, in fact, to the year or date of the birth of Jesus. There was no Nativity festival until the fourth century, when Christianity first became a permitted religion in the Roman Empire. The twenty-fifth day of December was chosen by these early converts because it was the peak of the rival festivities of sunworshipping pagans: the winter solstice.

The Saturnalia of the Romans was a time of debauchery and sacrifice, and this same impulse existed throughout Northern Europe at the dead of winter, when the sun, reaching its lowest ebb, died, and

Previous pages: A rare picture of the 'fuddles' – Manchester cotton workers celebrate Christmas in the factory. This kind of communal Christmas frolics was frowned upon by the Victorians

Opposite: The catalogue of Thomas Smith, inventor of the Christmas cracker, which helped turn pagan rituals into family fun

ESTAᴮ

THOMAS SMITH & CO

ILLUSTRATED CATALOGUE
OF

CHRISTMAS NOVELTIES

SEASON
1882-83

DRAWN BY C. H. TAFFS.

CRACKER-TIME AFTER DINNER.

was then reborn. The early Christians chose the rebirth of the Sun as the time for the birth of the Son of God. The confusion of impulses has been inherent in the festival ever since.

As Christianity spread through Europe, it had to contend with existing pagan rituals of native heathen populations, and quite deliberately set out to reinterpret many of them. Christmas carols had their origin in the pagan celebrations of the French peasantry, and in time were given Christian themes. The singing of carols in church was revived in the second half of the nineteenth century. The worship of evergreens – magical plants which did not die in winter – was given a Biblical meaning: the holly became the crown of thorns, and the red berry Christ's blood. This allowed for Christian missionaries to win over ordinary folk, who then decorated churches with quite un-Godly evergreens. But it also meant that there was a simmering conflict between the teachings of Christianity, and the older impulses of ordinary people to behave in quite an immoral way at Christmastime. When the Victorian revival of Christmas began in the early nineteenth century, many of the existing customs – such as the wassailing of apple trees, and the revelries associated with Twelfth Night – were blatantly raucous and ribald. Villagers let their hair down, got blind drunk, and threatened temporary social disorder. Men dressed up as women and women as men: fools were made kings.

During the nineteenth century, the Victorian middle classes sought to replace the old excesses with a new, demure, family-centred kind of Saturnalia. In this context, the invention and subsequent popularity of the Christmas cracker is absolutely crucial, though it appears now to be such a commonplace and banal device with its ridiculous punning jokes. Its history is one of the most bizarre in the story of the creation of the modern festival. In retrospect it was a brilliantly conceived device – the inspiration of a London sweet-maker, Tom Smith.

According to company legend, Tom Smith was first inspired to invent the cracker when he sat by his fire on Christmas Day wondering how on earth he could make his wrapped sweets sell at this time of year. He had introduced bon-bons from France quite successfully, and had put love notes and tokens in them to make them more attractive. But they would not sell at Christmas. He was struck – figuratively – by a spark from his log fire; as if he had found a key to the new festival, he had the idea that if he could make his wrapped sweets go bang, they

Opposite: A perfect illustration of the restrained Saturnalia encouraged by the Victorians and enjoyed here at an Edwardian Christmas

Overleaf: A family Christmas, 1936. By this time Christmas crackers were mass produced and available to middle-class families, though many still made their own

would sell at Christmas. He worked out how to make the controlled explosion, and his fire cracker sweets were almost immediately successful. They did even better when he added paper hats and trinkets.

It turned out that the Christmas cracker was tailor-made for the Victorian family Christmas dinner – a feeble spark which perfectly suited the demure sensibilities of the class, and mimicked the more ancient communal fire festivals which were rapidly disappearing from the scene. Once paper hats were added, it became the perfect little package of pagan ritual for the family table: fire and funny hats without the Saturnalian excesses.

In a way the cracker took some of the spark from another date in the Christmas calendar which remained important until the 1860s – Twelfth Night. In the middle ages, and right up to the eighteenth century, this was a time for a kind of ritualized riot in village communities, overseen by kings and queens elected for the occasion.

Twelfth Night lost much of its pagan vigour in the early nineteenth century, but retained in the Regency period a degree of ribaldry which clearly was not entirely to the taste of the Victorian middle classes – at least, not in the sacred setting of the family celebrations. In the 1790s, Twelfth Night cards were popular. These showed a caricature of a social type: Miss Frolic, Lady Racket, Lord Flirt Away, Tabatha

An example of Twelfth Night misrule in the early nineteenth century. Someone has tied the gentleman's coat tails to the lady's dress. Note the Twelfth cakes in the shop window

Tinderhart, Lady Dashall, and the like. These were used in games where the participants would take on the character of the joke person. There was often a rhyme with the card, such as:

> Miss Frolic spreads for hearts a snare
> She'll catch you if you don't take care.

Even in the 1840s, there were relatively risqué cards with riddles such as:

> Q: Why is Prince Albert liable to a military flogging from Queen Victoria?
> A: Because he is subject to her!

There was a raucousness, too, in the public celebrations of Twelfth Night – a bit like New Year's Eve nowadays. It was often a public holiday, and there were cheap cut-out characters in the broadsheets – popular newspapers of the time – depicting Twelfth Night characters. So the Miss Frolics and Lord Flirt Aways were known to quite a large section of the population. In the late 1820s, this description of the nonsenses of Twelfth Night was recorded in a book called *In London* by Thomas Hervey:

> Let all idle gazers in the streets of London, beware Twelfth Night! There is then, that spirit of mischief abroad which carried on without the superintending power of the Lord of Misrule, exhibits itself in the catching of the coat tails, of the unsuspecting passer-by, and fixing them to a nail, or such like as may be available on the frame of a door or window, where they might pause to gaze, and some other part to the garment of a person of the opposite sex, so neither can be freed.

This kind of Twelfth Night reflected the raucous and raffish world of the Regency, which died out by the middle of the century, to be replaced in middle-class households by naughty games, such as Blind Man's Buff, in which both children and adults participated. In the context of their own homes, the Victorians branded much of the fun and frolicking as childish. This was true of the once licentious habit of kissing under the mistletoe. In Dickens' *Sketches by Boz* of 1837 he describes a family Christmas, where grandpapa produces a small sprig of mistletoe from his pocket and tempts the young cousins to kiss under it. They are too young, it appears, for them to be anything but innocent.

A pagan survival – the fertility rites associated with mistletoe are retained in the Victorian custom of kissing under the mistletoe

Though the next example was written in 1913, there is an essentially Victorian feel to this 'agony aunt' piece in the *Home Companion* magazine about kissing under the mistletoe:

There is always a little laxity allowed at Christmas tide, for it is the time when gay spirits and rollicking laughter play a part, and young people will often have a little harmless flirtation under the mistletoe just for the fun of the thing.

Kissing under the mistletoe is a very old custom, and no girl should feel indignant or hurt if one of her admirers shows a keen desire to salute her in the way that Cupid so strongly approves.

Girls should remember that because a man wishes to kiss her under the mistletoe HE DOES NOT NECESSARILY MEAN TO PROPOSE TO HER!

Very often a man will purposely avoid kissing the girl to whom he is most attached in front of other people BECAUSE HE CONSIDERS HIS LOVE TOO SACRED FOR PUBLIC DISPLAY.

The restrained family celebrations of the middle classes contained many other references to more bawdy rituals once generally associated with Christmas. For example, it was quite common in parts of the country – at some time in the winter festivities – for men and women to swap clothes. This kind of role reversal was often associated with Twelfth Night.

The only references to this kind of thing in the middle-class family is the ritual of the head of the household being asked to help stir the Christmas pudding mixture. To refer again to *Sketches by Boz*, Dickens describes Uncle George, in whose house the gathering is held, going down to the kitchen to perform this task much to the amusement of the servants and everyone else. It was obviously quite something in the hierarchical Victorian family for such a figure to perform a menial task like that – an innocent example of what in other sections of society was known as 'topsy-turvy'.

The point was made in the last chapter that the middle-classes tried to encourage the working classes to adopt *their* kind of Christmas with missionary zeal. But it took a long time for these values to permeate the poor, and much more ribald versions of old village customs survived in urban working-class communities. In fact, the custom of 'topsy-turvy', where men dressed up as women and women as men, continued at Christmas until the 1940s in London's East End. From his childhood just before the Great War, Ted Harrison, the son of a night street sweeper, remembers:

After tea, Christmas night, the room was cleared. Uncles and aunts used to come round, and I used to like seeing them dress up. It was good to see her trying to get her bleeding boobs into his waistcoat, and big flabby behind trying to get into Uncle Joe's trousers. I know one of me uncles used to have a couple of pig's bladders I think they were, and put a little drop of water in 'em. He used to come in dancing and he'd chuck one over his shoulders, like that.

For middle-class Victorians, enjoyment of this kind had been transferred to the stage with the advent of the Pantomime. This had originally developed in the eighteenth century as a kind of mimed interlude in plays. Now, in a rather different guise, it reached a peak of popularity in the mid-Victorian period, when it first became associated specifically with Christmas. It is essentially a theatrical version of what were once common rituals in the essentially pagan celebrations of ordinary people. It was during this period that the convention arose of the principal boy being played by a girl, and the principal lady by a man. The Victorians turned the Pantomime into an entertainment to be enjoyed, despite its risqué jokes, by both children and adults.

Although, within the families of the working and middle classes, differences of behaviour survived for a very long time – as no doubt they still do – in the Victorian period the great distinction was between celebrations at home and in public, indoors and outdoors. Having drawn the Saturnalia to the cosiness of their comfortable hearths, the Victorian moralists abhorred the continuing community celebrations of the working class. In a leader published on Christmas Day 1877, *The Times* spluttered with indignation:

> Christmas is threatened by the multitude that choose to honour and observe it in their own way. There is no mincing the matter, nor is there disguising and no checking it either. Christmas for a large part of the people recalls the pagan Saturnalia without even the picturesque forms and social graces of paganism. The devotees reel about the streets, make nights hideous, turn their houses upside down, and crowd the police court . . . Christmas indoors and Christmas out of doors, are very different things. One class regards it as a very different thing. One class regards it

Topsy-turvy – the ritual in which men and women swapped clothes at Christmas – was once a tradition in London's East End. These are private photos from between the wars

One kind of misrule which died out in the nineteenth century – the 'waits', a tradition of street music, were banned in late Victorian times

A rare late Victorian illustration of what was once a common ritual – the schoolmaster 'barred out' by the boys before Christmas. He was only allowed to enter in exchange for a holiday

as a foretaste of heaven, the other is not capable of that sentiment, or that aspiration.

The legitimate excesses of the comfortably off were in eating, doling out goods to the poor, and present giving. The illegitimate excesses of the poorer people were in drinking, and filling the streets with noise. One well-established Christmas custom, banned by magistrates in late Victorian times, were the 'waits', when bands of poor amateur musicians would play in the streets. In the cotton mills of the North West workers enjoyed a Christmas frolic, known as 'the fuddles', in which there would be much drinking and what one contemporary described as 'wholesale kissing between the sexes'.

In institutions like the army and schools, older traditions of Christmas topsy-turviness and licence continued much longer. For example, it became a tradition in the services for officers to serve the men at Christmastime, and this still continues in some regiments.

Another tradition until the turn of the century was the ritual in which schoolboys would lock out the headmaster from school on one day of the year and bargain with him to get a holiday. This was called 'barring out'. It was recorded in Berwickshire, Scotland, in 1900 by John Mabbot who actually remembered 'bar-the-door day': 'It was a day when, all over Scotland, pupils arrived early and locked the headmaster out, whereupon, after certain ritual verses were exchanged, he and they all went home.'

Though this kind of topsy-turviness has declined with the gradual adoption by most of the population of the Christmas customs of the Victorians, it does still survive in various forms outside the home. There is, for example, a special licence at office parties to behave badly at Christmastime without any great fear of retribution. It is still quite acceptable in many hospitals, too, for the students and junior doctors to put on a Christmas review in which they satirize the consultants. These are not strictly ritualized events like 'barring out', but they do represent a survival – and possibly, in the case of the office party, a resurgence – of an old and not quite Victorian Christmas spirit.

One consistent theme in the topsy-turviness of Christmas which the Victorians did not do away with, but remodelled for an industrial society, was the impulse to treat the poor well, at least once a year. This has been called the 'Wenceslas Syndrome', after the Good King of the carol who sees a poor man gathering winter fuel and sets out to help him. The role played by charitable zeal in spreading the Christmas custom is explored in the next chapter.

Converting the Pauper

CHAPTER THREE

One Christmas morning I was in the workhouse infirmary feeling as if no one knew or cared for me when I found this letter on my pillow. I started! It might be to tell me my husband had died in the asylum, poor fellow. But no! There was just this letter and a beautiful card and I began to read it. And little by little the others woke up, and there was such a to-do! 'You got a letter Mrs H., I wish I had one.' And then one and another found a letter and a card; and they were so pleased; and it seemed a message from heaven, it did.

This was one of the testimonials collected by a long-forgotten late Victorian charity – the Christmas Letter Mission. It began in Brighton in 1871 when a small band of church-going ladies decided to send a Christmas card and an accompanying letter to anyone unlucky enough to be spending Christmas Day in hospital in Sussex. Ten years later this small band had become a national organization which every year sent a personal Christmas message to the inmates of practically every workhouse, refuge, hospital, infirmary, and prison in Britain – a total of around 300,000 people. Each envelope was marked 'A Christmas Letter for You', and was usually placed beside every inmate's pillow by a member of staff after dark on Christmas Eve. The Christmas Card Mission was one of the many Victorian charities which introduced the poor to the new Christmas ritual. In so doing they played a major role in promoting the modern middle-class ideal of Christmas, and spreading it to the mass of the population who knew little of it and could not afford it.

The story of the promotion of the new Christmas by zealous ladies and gentlemen is best charted through Victorian newspapers and magazines. It is quite extraordinary to find that in almost every newspaper from the weighty *Times* down to the popular illustrated weeklies, there is practically no reference to Christmas at all during the first three decades of the nineteenth century, and few until the 1850s. Christmas Eve, Christmas Day, and Boxing Day come and go just like any other day. Although you find the occasional advertisement for presents or poultry, Victorian entrepreneurs were clearly slow in

Previous pages: The Victorian ideal of Christmas was first spread by charity. This is a scene from the Farnborough Institute, 1934

exploiting the commercial potential of the event. What is striking, however, is the gradual emergence of a kind of Christmastide culture of benevolence towards the poor which starts to take off from the 1840s onwards. Appeals for funds to help destitute children, sewing classes to make Christmas gifts of warm clothes for the deserving poor, and 'doles' of bread and money for the aged, all start to appear in the run up to 25 December. There are regular features on the visits of charitable ladies and local grandees to workhouses, reformatories and prisons, together with descriptions of poor people banqueting on roast beef and plum pudding. The Boxing Day issue of *The Times* in 1877, for example, reported:

Cow Cross Mission [in London] collected one hundred and fifty little mudlarks to act as beefeaters on Christmas day. They were arranged according to sex at two long tables on which were knives and forks, water cups, and hunks of bread. In less than a couple of minutes the whole of the bread was eaten. Immediately afterwards large joints of beef and pork were brought in and great sieves of potatoes. These were soon cut up by half a dozen carvers, with numbers of ladies and gentlemen acting as waiters. There was no stint of either meat or plum pudding, everyone being allowed to come as often as he or she liked, and many sly bits of meat and pudding were slipped into pinafores and caps to take home.

Middle-class ladies played a key role in bringing Christmas to the poor. They feature prominently in reports of the thousands of church-visiting societies, moral reform unions and benevolent funds which did so much Christmas charity work in the second half of the nineteenth century. Promoting the new Christmas, with its sentimental image of the happy family and contented children, was a cause close to the heart of many Victorian ladies with time on their hands. And any backslider could expect a severe reprimand, if only in the pages of women's journals whose Christmas issues from the 1870s onwards often stressed the importance of doing one's new annual duty to the poor.

The positive image that was held up for ladies of leisure to aspire to was that of the harmonious and rather idyllic village community in which the bonds of duty between rich and poor were cemented each Christmas by the benevolence of the local 'gentry'. There was also lots

Overleaf: One scene from a charitable Christmas. The Church Army gives a party for poor children in 1912. The founder, Wilson Carlile, lies down amongst his flock

of practical advice on how to organize 'treats' for the poor and make personalized presents for them. One article on Christmas treats which appeared in *The Lady* in December 1906 began:

> 'I got this beautiful warm cross-over at the last treat,' says old Widow Brown, 'and my lady worked it with her own hands, "for," says she, "I've made a bright red border to it, knowing how you like a bit of colour." And the year before I had the loveliest petticoat, and little Missie at the Grange made me a pair of scarlet mittens.'
>
> Those who live in villages will be well acquainted with such conversations as this, for they know that the Christmas treat to the poor folk is the great event of the year to them, and one which furnishes the favourite topic of talk and thought for the ensuing twelve months. It is not the amount of money spent on these festivities which make them so delightful to the humble guests, but the trouble which is taken to ensure a happy evening, and the care with which each individual is provided with a gift which will be just what she wants.

One of the inspirations for this great wave of benevolence at Christmas was Charles Dickens' *A Christmas Carol*, first published in 1843. He originally intended to write a moral tract on the injustices of poverty and inequality after a visit to the textile mills of Manchester. Then he decided that a story which used the sentimental associations of the Christmas season would get his message over more powerfully. Dickens' moving tale of Scrooge's conversion to the spirit of Christmas was – as Dickens intended – read as an indictment of the neglect of the poor in the new industrial towns and cities. It touched the conscience of the Victorian middle classes and was a huge commercial success: 15,000 copies were sold in its first year, and it was dramatized for special Christmas performances in theatres all over Britain. It was appealing because it promoted a ritual which seemed as if it might help heal the growing division and conflict between the classes – a recurrent fear in the nineteenth century. It was a re-working of an age-old aristocratic custom of giving alms to the poor at this time of the year which – it was popularly imagined – was part of the stable social fabric of 'Merrie Olde Englande'.

The new middle-class fashion for charity giving at Christmas also gradually replaced another old tradition – that of giving a Christmas Box. For centuries masters and householders had given gifts of money to those who served them, and tradesmen had rewarded loyal customers with free goods. Those collecting from house to house, carried boxes, which is the probable origin of the term Boxing Day. This trans-action usually took place on 26 December. But from the 1830s onwards this tradition began to be heavily criticized every Christmas in the press. It was claimed that the custom was abused by unscrupulous members of the 'servant' class. Every Boxing Day many householders were invaded by a small army of postmen, sweeps, street sweepers, and tradesmen's servants requesting money. Failure to pay held the threat of reduced efficiency in the service that was provided in the following year. Many tradesmen also claimed that they had to spend a small fortune on free gifts in order to 'hold' their customers for another year. From the 1850s onwards many tradesmen followed the example of the shop keepers of Pembroke Dock who in 1855 'determined to abolish the custom of giving Christmas Boxes to their customers and have had a meeting and issued an address to that effect'. And the practice of giving Christmas boxes to 'servants' was also eclipsed around this time by the new fashion for charity giving. The Victorian middle classes wanted to promote themselves as guardians of the poor, and the money which might have been spent on Christmas boxes often found its way into charity boxes.

One curious consequence of the charitable zeal with which some middle-class people took the new Christmas to the poor and to the Victorian underworld was that on Christmas Day itself the inmates of a prison or a workhouse might enjoy more food and festivities than the working-class families outside. In the 1860s *The Hereford Times*, for example, recorded how three hundred or so inmates of Hereford workhouse regularly received Christmas cards, Christmas presents of oranges, tobacco, and sweets, and a Christmas dinner of roast beef and plum pudding. They were also treated to a magic lantern show, a carol service, and a 'turn' by the local vicar who 'sang several capital songs, accompanying himself on the piano'. In the Christmas speech the inmates at Hereford, as in so many other workhouses, were told by the Chairman of the Board of Guardians, that on this day they were 'better off than the poor people outside' – a fact that was most probably true. The trappings of the modern Christmas – the Christmas meal, the Christmas presents, the Christmas tree, and so on – probably reached the lowest levels of society before they reached the mass of the working classes. A docker or a horse bus driver might well have heard of the new craze for Christmas from a grandfather in the local workhouse or from a sick relative in an infirmary. For some of the Christmas celebrations in workhouses were spectacular – at least by the standards of the day – and must have created a deep and lasting impression amongst the inmates and their friends and relatives. In January 1864, for example, *The Illustrated London News* reported a

Christmas celebrations in Greenwich workhouse, 1864. The boom in Victorian charities meant that inmates often enjoyed the trappings of the new Christmas before their poor families and friends outside

grand Christmas entertainment at the Greenwich workhouse in south London. Interestingly, it was held on the eve of Twelfth Night, and the presents given were described as 'New Year's gifts' – both throwbacks to an earlier tradition when the festivities were spread out over the twelve days of Christmas and not all concentrated on Christmas Day:

Through the liberality of Mrs Angerstein, wife of the member of Greenwich, the inmates of the Union House in that town were, on the 5th inst., brought together in the great hall to commemorate the beginning of the new year. . . . A scene never before witnessed within the walls of the Union House was the result. Between 900 and 1,000 of the inmates, men, women and children – not excluding the imbecile and the insane – assembled in the dining hall. The hall was tastefully decorated with flags, lent for the occasion by Captain Lane of Greenwich; whilst at the head of it, in front of which gas-jets ran, raised on a stand, were eight magnificent Christmas trees, the two centre reaching to the ceiling, about 12 ft. high, and the whole being laden with prizes –

toys for the children, and small bags of snuff, tobacco, and tea for the old people. The eight trees bore on their illuminated branches three thousand of these New Year gifts.

Christmas probably also quickly came to be the highlight of the year for most inmates of Victorian prisons. The following (edited) description of Christmas in gaol, written by 'one long since released' appeared in *Chambers Journal* in December 1879. It refers back to the 1840s or 50s and, to our knowledge, is the only detailed, first-hand account of a prison Christmas in early Victorian Britain:

The happy day had come which was to give us some change from the diet we had been living upon so long; and though it was only one meal extra, still it was known to be such as many outside would be glad to jump at. In fact this was the anniversary of roast beef, potatoes and beer, to be served out to the prisoners in addition to the usual allowances; and most eagerly was the day looked for weeks previously. The customary allowance was served out at noon, so that the extra Christmas fare should be a supplementary meal at 2 p.m. What we had for the common food at twelve o'clock was the usual bread and soup, nothing more. This was hardly touched by anyone. Then began our preparations for the great feast. The table was neatly laid; plates and knives and forks were placed in good order; and the chimes of a neighbouring clock outside were impatiently listened to as we counted the quarter hours. At length the quarter hour before two sounded, and then we saw come down from a huge wicker concern, lined with tin, and called the bread basket. This was filled with the best, or so considered best, white bread and a pound of it was served out to each man. By the time this was done the church clock outside struck two, and then several large tin dishes laden with separate allowances of the baked beef and potatoes appeared. The sight and smell of them were almost a feast in themselves, for nothing of the kind had we caught glimpse of for many a long day. Each of us soon had a pound of solid good beef, the same quantity of potatoes, and a pint of porter. The health of those who had given us this treat was pledged in a manner which no one need have been ashamed of. It may seem strange to say so, and yet hungry as we had felt, not one in the ward could manage the whole quantity of meat belonging to him. I was satisfied before half had been eaten, and consequently reserved a portion for my supper and the next day. In our ward it was found that with our ordinary food added, we had a sufficiency to last us comfortably for three days. The afternoon was spent in talking and walking, and at supper our gruel was scarcely touched. How could it be the horrid stuff, after such a 'feast for the Gods' as we had but just enjoyed!

The boom in benevolence towards the very poor every December helped to create a strange social 'problem' which emerged each Christmas. By the mid-Victorian period there were so many Christmas charities in the big cities, they acted as a magnet for casual labourers, the unemployed, tramps, and travelling criminals from far and wide. Those who were desperate or down on their luck clamoured to take advantage of the 'open door' policy of hostels, night refuges, asylums, missions, and workhouses, and enjoy the free meals and parcels of tea, sugar, flour and coal that were offered to the needy. Also, at Christmastime there was a new atmosphere of generosity towards people seen begging on the streets, nicely summed up in the Victorian children's nursery rhyme:

> Christmas is coming, the goose is getting fat,
> Please put a penny in the old man's hat.

London was the most popular city for this midwinter migration, for it was the home of almost 1,000 charities by the late nineteenth century, supported by private subscription or the rates, many of which had special Christmas funds. For the army of 30,000 or more people who tramped into London to spend the coldest winter months in town, Christmas was the high point of the poor man's 'season'.

What made this 'season' irresistible for many poor people was the fact that, in addition to the bounty of charity handouts, there was also a growing mass of odd jobs they could pick up in the weeks before Christmas. As the 'commercial' Christmas took off especially from the 1870s onwards, extra hands were taken on all over London: in the Post Office to deal with the rush of Christmas mail; at the railway stations to cope with the increase in traffic; in the theatres to shift scenery and parade around the streets with boards advertising panto-mimes; and on the streets to distribute handbills promoting trades-men's wares. Also some migrants would go street hawking, selling holly, mistletoe, and cheap Christmas trees – some of which were regularly collected or stolen on the journey into the capital.

A magic lantern slide show from the 1880s with a temperance theme showing how drinking can lead to destitution. The Christmas crusade was partly inspired by a desire to replace excessive drinking at Christmastime with a respectable family festival in the home

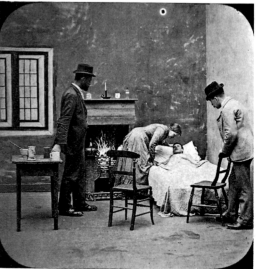

This 'season' was the first sign that the spirit of Christmas promoted by Dickens, in which the rich remembered their duty to the poor, was not so easy to achieve as was first imagined. In the eyes of some it was all starting to go dreadfully wrong. It was feared in certain quarters – including sections of the church – that respectable working-class folk would be demoralized by the midwinter wealth and Christmas revelling of the casual poor, and follow them along a path of drunkenness and debauchery. According to the Bishop of London in 1870, this benevolence 'instead of relieving human misery, increases vice and begging for the impostors find it very easy to have different places of abode and receive three, four or five family allowances from the various agencies'. In a sermon on Christmas dinners quoted in *The Times* on Christmas Day, 1877, the Rev. W. Hodgson claimed that 'the Christmas dinner of my family costs less per head than most of these charity dinners. Every dinner which exceeds a shilling is a waste and no tea to children ought to cost more than fivepence a head at this season.' From the 1870s onwards the handouts were rationed and often means-tested by a new agency backed by many churches – the Charity Organization Society. This, combined with shrinking unemployment, greatly reduced the seasonal migration into the metropolis, but complaints of 'uninvited Christmas guests feasting at the expense of London ratepayers' continued in *The Times* until the end of the century.

Although Christmas remained the best day of the year in institutions, and inmates probably continued to enjoy more of the trappings than poor families outside, there was a new atmosphere in Christmas charities during the late Victorian and Edwardian period. The old Dickensian dream of 'good will to all men' was replaced by a more austere approach. Christmas was used as a festival to encourage moral reform and reward the respectable poor. Most charities began to restrict their 'gifts' to families who were 'deserving': church attendance, cleanliness and temperance all scored points in your favour, while drunkenness or disorderly behaviour counted strongly against you. By the end of the nineteenth century some charities claimed to have social workers who checked the authenticity of every family who received their Christmas parcels. Christmas charity dinners became punctuated with sermons and speeches, some of which blamed the poverty of the guests on their own imprudence and bad habits. For example, on Christmas Day 1883 *The Times* summarized a speech made the night before by Mr Bourke, the member for King's Lynn, at the distribution of Christmas dinners for the poor of Homerton and Hackney Wick:

Addressing those present he said that latterly much had been heard about the great destitution that prevailed in the East End of London and the public had been aroused to do the best it could to alleviate the distress. But all the efforts of legislation and all the efforts of public men would be of little use if the people did not try to help themselves. They could not shut their eyes to the fact – uncomfortable and unpalatable as it might be – that a large portion of the existing misery was unfortunately brought on the people by themselves. They must cease from drunkenness and vice.

The most hostile Christmas messages on record were those delivered by the Navvy Mission Society whose purpose was to save the souls of one of the toughest, most hard-drinking and irreligious group of workers thrown up by Victorian society – the railway navvies. The Rev. D. W. Barrett's Christmas message for 1878 was:

1. Have you prayed much to God during the year?
2. Have you read your Bible very often?
3. Have you been as often as you ought, or at all, to a place of worship?
4. Have you or have you not made yourself like one of the beasts that perish by the sin of drunkenness?
5. Have you been a swearing man?
6. Sisters, what about your lives? Have they been the lives of Christian women?

Perhaps you will be killed suddenly by a fall of earth, by the blasting of a rock, by the crunching blow of an engine, by a bruise which may fester, and mortify, and poison the life blood, by a fall, by the slow torture of disease, or by the burning heat of fever . . . But however it may be, or where it may happen, let me ask you, are you ready now? Shall you be ready to meet death then?

In the workhouse inmates now had to earn their Christmas dinner with stints of granite breaking in the newly opened stone yards. And their traditional jug of Christmas beer was banned from 1884 onwards as a result of the agitation of the Workhouse Drink Reform League. In the late Victorian years the inmates had to toast the health of the Queen and the workhouse master with water. The increasing austerity which lay behind the Christmas festivities in the workhouse was parodied by George Sims in his sentimental poem 'In the Workhouse: Christmas Day', published in 1877. The workhouse Christmas charity is too little, too late, to save the life of the wife of the poem's main character, the pauper John, and she dies of starvation.

The poem begins:

> It is Christmas Day in the workhouse,
> And the cold bare walls are bright
> With garlands of green and holly,
> And the place is a pleasant sight:
> For with clean-washed hands and faces,
> In a long and hungry line
> The paupers sit at the tables,
> For this is the hour they dine.
>
> And the guardians and their ladies,
> Although the wind is east,
> Have come in their furs and wrappers,
> To watch their charges feast;
> To smile and be condescending,
> Put pudding on paupers' plates,
> To be hosts at the workhouse banquet
> They've paid for with the rates.
>
> Oh, the paupers are meek and lowly
> With their 'Thank 'ee kindly mum's';
> So long as they fill their stomachs,
> What matters it whence it comes?
> But one of the old men mutters,
> And pushes his plate aside:
> 'Great God!' he cries, 'but it chokes me!
> For this is the day she died.'

This kind of workhouse Christmas is still just within the grasp of living memory. Gina Baker remembers spending Christmas Day in the Paddington workhouse in 1905, when she was eight:

Christmas Day we got up at six o'clock in the morning and we had to wash and dress. Our uniform was blue bloomers and a serge dress with a coloured pinafore. After washing, we had to strip our beds, then we were ready for breakfast. The breakfast consisted of bread and dripping and cocoa. After breakfast we had to do the chores that were ours every day; it didn't make no difference that it was Christmas Day, we still had to do it. My chore was scrubbing the tables. After that we had to go back to our rooms and make the bed. Then we came down and were given a Christmas dinner, which on this occasion happened to be turkey with the usual vegetables and Christmas pudding. This being Christmas Day, we'd been told if we behaved ourselves we were going to get a present from Father Christmas. So when dinner was over we retired to the recreation room, there we had to line up in twos to be taken onto the platform to receive a present from Father Christmas who was one of the governors dressed up. Well, I was given a present and mine was a white pinafore with lace epaulettes on the shoulders, and I was proud of that pinafore but you were only allowed to wear it on a Sunday.

The new austerity at Christmas was usually directed more towards adults than children. At parties for children of the poor, or at Christmas celebrations in children's homes, there seems to have been a strong desire to indulge underprivileged children and make them happy – at least for one day of the year. This was one expression of the increasing extent to which Christmas was becoming a children's festival. The Christmas issue of the Salvation Army's *Social Gazette* for 1900 reported how volunteers made a determined effort to give the slum children of London a happy Christmas by organizing Christmas tree parties for them – thus earning for themselves the nickname 'the Christmas Tree Harmy':

> In twenty of the slummiest districts of London nearly three thousand of the poorest of children have experienced the delight of gazing upon a Christmas tree, and receiving some gifts from its toy laden boughs. . . . Poor mites! One cannot look upon them, even in their merriment, without a pang of sorrow as one realises that all the glitter and brightness of this occasion is as a fleeting flash of sunlight, that relieves only for a moment the black winter of their young lives. For the moment, at any rate, thank God! the little ones had forgotten the fireless attic and coverless bed, and were standing around the Christmas tree in a very intoxication of merriment. . . . The day following, the slum children marched about, filling the air with the sound of trumpet and mouth-organ. The girls paraded the courts with their new dolls, and thus they continued the rejoicing of the previous night. One little mite expressed the pent-up feelings of the rest by saying, as she hugged her dolly to her: 'Oh sister! Wasn't it grand?'

A spirit of child-centred benevolence also transformed the atmosphere of the Dr Barnardo's Village Home for orphans and pauper children at Barkingside, Essex, on Christmas Day. G. V. Holmes, in her autobiography *The Likes of Us*, described her Christmases there as a child from 1910 onwards:

No one who has ever visited the Village on Christmas Day can ever forget the experience. No children, the richest or most beloved, could have a happier, jollier time than we enjoyed at Christmas. Never did grown up people work harder, or with the greater understanding than the staff we knew. It was indeed the Children's Day. . . . [on Christmas Day] the sound we had been listening for at last reached us. The procession was coming! Into sight came a marching band – blowing their silvery notes across the cold air. Then came the sound of cart wheels, and, round the bend, came a horse-drawn cart beautifully decorated and filled with sacks of toys, followed by other carts filled with sacks; but the greatest thrill of all was when a real Father Christmas stepped onto our concrete and delivered personally to us a sack of toys. The oldest girls stepped forward to receive it, whilst Father Christmas shook hands, or patted heads, or beat a hasty retreat if any of the smaller ones began screaming with fright. We cheered Father Christmas as he made his way onwards. It was one of the workmen, usually the head gardener, who performed this rite.

After the Great War there was a renewed drive to make Christmas a time to remember, not just for children but for everyone in need. Every Christmastime countless thousands of well-intentioned people – and in the fore would be middle-class ladies – devoted part of their Christmas to organizing treats for the needy at local workhouses, refuges, orphanages, children's homes, and hospitals. Christmas was seen – as it had been now for almost a century – as a time to help those worse off than yourself. At the parties laid on for the poor and the sick, Union Jacks were often draped everywhere – evidence that the charitable zeal was closely tied up with a new sense of national unity and social duty generated by the war. Yet even the best-intentioned Christmas charities sometimes backfired, due often to a lack of sensitivity towards the needs of the people they were trying to help. Lil Hemmings was one of the children who, every Christmas just after the war, received a free pair of boots from the Lord Mayor of Bristol's Boot Fund, set up to provide for the poor children of fathers fighting at the Front:

They were great big working men's boots with steel caps on them, and you had to queue up for them just before Christmas. Mother made me go. I hated them; they were so painful they'd bring my feet out in blisters. And the other children used to make fun of you

The Salvation Army brings Christmas to slum children in London, 1900

at school for wearing them because everyone knew they were charity boots. I was so ashamed of them once or twice I stayed away from school especially. But what I did was to ride along hanging on to the backs of carts, and dig the boot into the road so that the sparks did fly. That way they only lasted a couple of weeks then they had holes in them. So I used to get rid of them pretty quick.

The determination to help, or at least to try to help, those in need at Christmas was given a further urgency by the deprivations caused by the Second World War and which continued into the austerity years of the 1950s. But greater affluence and the development of the welfare state started to reduce much of the need for charitable efforts at Christmas. More poor people could afford to pay for a proper Christmas for themselves, and those in institutions were now provided for by the state, not just by charity workers. It is hard not to read into the countless attacks on the recent commercialism of Christmas a sense of loss amongst the middle classes, because they no longer have the opportunity ritually to give to those beneath them in the social scale, as they did in the past. From the viewpoint of the charity workers who played such an important role in spreading the Christmas ideal, it has gone disastrously wrong. What started out as a public ritual to restore a better relationship between the haves and have-nots, has turned into one in which families eat and drink themselves to excess in the privacy of their own homes.

Nevertheless, charity work and consideration for others continue to be a part, though now a minor part, of the Christmas ethos. Most recently this spirit of benevolence has been given a new lease of life by young people raising money for the poor Third World countries at Christmas. The most notable example has been Band Aid's hit record of 1984 'Do They Know It's Christmas?', the proceeds of which went to the Ethiopian Relief Fund. However, the heyday of Christmas charity work was in the second half of the nineteenth century, and it played a pioneering role in bringing Christmas to all classes of society.

Winning hearts and minds. Above: An Edwardian Christmas scene in Great Ormond Street Hospital for children in London. Below: A charitable Christmas dinner with ear-splitting accompaniment in the 1930s

Home for the Holiday

CHAPTER FOUR

It was the Victorians who made Christmas the festival of the family and created the compulsion people still feel today to get home for Christmas. But, as with every other aspect of the modern Christmas, it was only the middle classes who could fulfil their own ideal of the family reunion. For a long time, as the propagandists of the new Christmas encouraged a popular acceptance of this ideal, the conditions in which the mass of people lived made it quite impossible for them to have family reunions at this time of the year. It does not seem to have struck as contradictory even such an astute social observer as Charles Dickens that while the middle classes extolled the virtue of the Christmas family reunion, their own celebrations required an army of servants who were necessarily kept from their own families. Because there was so much work to do at Christmastime, most domestic servants were needed to keep the household going. This was a considerable number of people: in 1911 1,400,000 people were employed in service, most of whom would be cooking and clearing up someone else's Christmas dinner. Jack Gosney was a young footman serving the Digby family at Sherborne Castle, Dorset, during the Great War. He remembers the hard work Christmas meant for the staff:

On Christmas morning we started off the same as any other morning. I got up about a quarter past, half past six, thanks to the old alarm clock, and got busy with taking the lamps down to be refilled, and cleaned as usual the boots of the family and any visitors that were there. My job was to see to the fires and the Christmas tree, do the washing up for the dinner, see the silver safely stored away and clear the table, which would often be hanging about till nine, because if there were any gentlemen circulating the port we were still waiting to put the finishing touch. Then I'd wash up and place the candles for them to go to bed before 10.30 p.m., and that was the Christmas come and gone.

Previous pages: The boom in boarding schools in the nineteenth century provided a great impetus for the middle-class Christmas home-coming

Opposite, above: Lord Bath in his Edwardian childhood at Longleat House, Wiltshire, a time when forty-three servants looked after the need of family and guests at Christmas
Below: Edwardian farm servants in Northumberland. The middle-class family Christmas depended on an army of domestics who could not go home to their own family celebrations

"WARM RECEPTION." MUGGLESWICK, 1917.

The Victorian ideal: the family gathered round the hearth on Christmas Day. A painting by Walter Denby Sadler

Servants were, in a sense, an integral part of the household – it was their home as well – and though they might not be able to join their own families, they were as a rule given special treatment at Christmas. The 6th Marquis of Bath recalls the festive atmosphere during Christmas before the Great War at Longleat House in Wiltshire, which then had forty-three servants:

I slept on the second floor and the staff slept above me and during the evenings I used to hear running about going on up there. I thought it was ghosts, but I later discovered it was a footman chasing a housemaid. On the other hand, they might have to work seven days a week, as required, and at Christmastime I can't remember any of the staff being allowed to go home and see their parents or their families, which they would probably do to-day. . . .

The servants had a dance, that was the most extraordinary thing, because they used to dance in the courtyard and that's open to the elements – why they weren't all frozen to death I don't know – and a band used to come down and play and if it was snowing it was just bad luck. Again, on Christmas Eve we had another dance in the dining room for the sort of upper strata of servants; the housekeepers, the house steward, the butler, the head cook, and all that sort of thing. My mother used to dance with the house steward and my father with the housekeeper to start the thing going, and I think on the whole they had a good time.

It was not just in the great houses that servants had to stay at work, away from their own families at Christmas. In middle-class homes there were no balls to attend, but servants were often treated as one of the family – at least for that one special day of Christmas – which must have made being away from home slightly easier to bear. Betty Ward from Jarrow in Northumberland remembers, almost as if it were a fairy tale, the kindness of her London employers during her first Christmas away from home in 1935:

I was in service in London with a lovely family, and of course Christmas came around but I never thought of it as a Christmas because I was away from home. I just took things normal, did my work and went to bed – just like an ordinary night, not like Christmas Eve. Then after I'd been asleep for quite a while, I think, I woke up and I thought, 'There's a knock on the door' and I said, 'Come in.' And it was the master and the mistress and the daughter with a glass of sherry and a piece of cake, and we drank the sherry, wished one another a Merry Christmas and they said 'These are for you, Betty' and there were some presents and there was one from the dog with a paw mark on it!

The most humble domestic servants were not, as a rule, ungrateful to their employers, for they at least got a decent Christmas dinner, often more than they could have expected at home. But for young girls being in a strange family at Christmas was also heartbreaking. Rose Ashton of Barrow-in-Furness spent her first Christmas as a maid in 1907 when she was only twelve years old. She was on a farm in the Lake District:

> They were very good to me and very kind. We had our Christmas dinner, and I washed up. Then I came in and she said, 'Have you finished, Rose?' I said, 'Yes, madam.' She said, 'Well, there's a ball of string there, and there's a pile of paper and a pair of scissors. I want you to go down to the paddock.' Now the paddock was the toilet and it was a long way from the farm yard, and I sat there cutting these papers and threading them with the needle to hang on the toilet door. They were very good and very kind to me, but I cried buckets of tears. I was crying all the while I was cutting these papers thinking about me mam and the others at Christmas, and me sitting there.

Many domestics around the time of the Great War must have felt a longing to get home, or at least a pang of remorse that they could not be with their families during the festive season. What seems extraordinary today is that just half a century before, this impulse to be reunited with the family at Christmas hardly existed at all either amongst domestic servants or industrial workers. Poorer people did have family reunions but they usually had nothing to do with Christmas.

The transformation of Britain from an agricultural to an industrial nation in the nineteenth century had in a sense created the need for a family reunion festival by encouraging so many people to leave their old family homes and move to the booming towns to look for work. Most sons and daughters who left home in search of a new life usually travelled a relatively short distance to the nearest town or city – often less than thirty miles – and were thus close enough to return to see their parents at least once a year.

However, this growing industrial army did not at first choose Christmas as the time to take a holiday and go home. Most would have

The hiring fair at Stratford-on-Avon, 1907. In rural areas summer festivals like this continued to be the main time for family reunions until the Great War

had to walk home and if the weather was bad many country roads became treacherous or impassable by midwinter. It made more sense to walk or hitch a lift home on a cart in the summer months when the days were longer and warmer, and when the roads were safe. Consequently, during the nineteenth century, traditional festivals like the Michaelmas hiring fairs, the Wakes Weeks in the North, and the Whitsun revels and feasts in the South and South East increasingly became occasions for family homecomings and reunions. As one old East Anglian farm worker, recalling family life in late Victorian times, told pioneer oral historian George Ewart Evans: 'We didn't go much for Christmas, Christmas Day fared to be like a Sunday; and apart from the bit of fun for the children there was not much a-doing. It was at Whitsun we had our holiday: then we enjoyed ourselves right well.'

The Wakes, which were very common all over Lancashire, Yorkshire, Cheshire, and Staffordshire, were short summer holidays when all the factories, mills, or mines in a particular town or village would close down. Travelling fairs moved in to provide the main entertainment and excitement for the local revellers. Each town would hold their Wakes at a different time, and many of their new citizens would take advantage of the break to go back *en masse* to wherever they had come from. The middle years of the nineteenth century were the heyday of the Wakes as family festivals, with much feasting, drinking, and an 'open house' atmosphere. *The Manchester Examiner* described Wakes Sunday in Oldham in 1846 as an event in which 'thousands of well-dressed working men and women wend their way to and from the dwellings of their relatives and friends'. Christmas, in comparison, was a tame and insignificant event for many working people in the North. In Bolton in the 1860s, for example, there was virtually no recognition of Christmas Day whatsoever, and mills and shops opened as usual. New Year's Day, by comparison, was 'the' midwinter feast day all over Lancashire, but it was not associated with going home.

The fashion for going home at Christmas originated very much within the middle classes. The ideal of the family reunion at Christmas began to gain currency in Christmas editions of magazines and newspapers during the 1840s. An early and typically sentimental statement of this new midwinter fashion appeared in *The Illustrated London News* of 1849. Headlined 'MEETING OF FAMILIES AT CHRIST-MAS' it began:

> One of the greatest pleasures Christmas brings is the assembling of members of families – the bringing together once more of all the old familiar faces around the household hearth. To see the venerable father and mother still occupying their old armchairs; to sit at the same place at the table which they formerly claimed as their own, beside the sister with whom they once kissed and quarrelled a dozen times a day, yet loved all the more after each childish squabble – these are the little home touches that send a silent thrill through the heart, and force tears into the eyes unawares.

One frequent theme in this early literature about Christmas was that of the schoolboy coming home for the Christmas holiday. This suggests that the growth of the public school system in the nineteenth century provided one last impetus for the development of the middle-class Christmas homecoming. The Christmas holiday took on great sentimental significance as a time of reunion between children and parents. This Christmas homecoming both reflected and reinforced the growing trend towards Christmas becoming a children's festival. We know that reunions of parents and pupils took place in previous centuries, but they became more important in the nineteenth century as the public schools grew into a major national institution through which tens of thousands of pupils passed each year. These new public schools favoured the boarding system, whereas in the past day pupils had been a more popular option in many private and endowed schools. One of the earliest and most evocative descriptions of the schoolboy's coach journey home appears in *Old Christmas* (first published in 1821), written by Washington Irving, an American friend of Charles Dickens:

> I had three fine rosy cheeked schoolboys for my fellow-passengers inside, full of the buxom health and manly spirit which I have observed in the children of this country. They were returning home for the holidays in high glee, and promising themselves a world of enjoyment. It was delightful to hear the gigantic plans of pleasure of the little rogues, and the impracticable feats they were to perform during their six weeks' emancipation from the abhorred thraldom of books, birch and pedagogue. They were full of anticipation of the meeting with the family and the household, down to the very cat and dog; and of the joy they were to give their little sisters by the presents with which their pockets were crammed; but the meeting to which they seemed to look forward with the greatest impatience was with Bantam, which I found to be a pony, according to their talk, possessed of more virtues than and steed since the days of Bucephalus.

The middle classes chose Christmas rather than a sunny season for their grand family reunion probably because of a renewed interest among Christians in the nineteenth century with the story of Jesus's life, and the Nativity in particular. Though the Nativity play had been common in the New Testament story for illiterate audiences, it was the death and resurrection theme of Easter which was considered more important in the belief of Christians before the Victorian revival of Christmas. Renewed interest in the Nativity, and the classic family scene of the Crib, coincided with the middle-class dependence on the family.

The family was important to the middle classes as the best way of binding people together economically and emotionally in an industrial society which tore apart community ties. For they too experienced a fragmentation of family ties as fathers and sons pursued careers in the growing towns and cities of the railway age. The most powerful magnet of all was London, with its great concentration of banks, insurance companies, and government offices. Because they were better off, most could afford a railway ticket to go home for Christmas – and this they did increasingly. This exodus home was given a further boost by the growing practice amongst managers and senior office staff of taking Boxing Day as a holiday from the mid nineteenth century onwards. The Bank Holiday Acts of the 1870s extended this practice to more lowly clerks by giving formal recognition to the lengthening of the Christmas holiday to include Boxing Day in banks, public offices, and stock exchanges.

The railways played an important part in promoting the custom of going home for Christmas and making possible the Christmas family reunion. In the 1912 edition of the *Railway Magazine* there is a mammoth piece of historical research which calculated the increase in passenger traffic over Christmas week during the period 1861 to 1912. All the companies reported substantial increases in Christmas traffic over the previous fifty years. The Midland, Caledonian, Great Northern, and Great Western Railway Companies, for example, carried around five times the volume of passengers they had before. Part of this increase was due to the extension of the railway network which more than doubled in size during this period. But two of the main factors which contributed to the upsurge in Christmas traffic were cheaper fares and the speeding up of journeys, particularly at Christmas. Rival companies battled to carry passengers home faster than each other on their steam-powered Christmas expresses and excursions. One way of doing this was by running non-stop trains between major cities. The 'journey shrinkage' between 1861 and 1912 is very impressive. The journey time from London to Aberdeen at Christmas time was reduced from 18 hours in 1861 to 11½ in 1912; and from London to Liverpool was reduced from 5½ hours in 1861 to 4 hours in 1912. With people having such a short Christmas holiday – usually just two or three days – the speed of the journey was a key factor in determining whether it was possible or worthwhile to go home at all.

It was really only in the last quarter of the nineteenth century that the habit of going home for Christmas began to take root in working-class communities, and even then it was a slow process. There was no tradition of poorer people going home at this time of the year earlier in the century because they had to work on Christmas Day. The demands of the factory age, with its regimented labour force, had more or less obliterated the age-old observance, common in country areas, of a midwinter holiday. The only holidays which the Factory Act of 1833 prescribed for children under twelve in the textile mills, for example, were Christmas Day and Good Friday, and even then there was a

Overleaf: In the 1930s passengers on some Christmas excursion trains sat in decorated carriages and enjoyed festive food

loophole whereby children could work on Christmas Day if they wanted to. Many families chose to do this because an enforced holiday without pay left them without food and fuel.

All this started to change later in the century, partly as a result of the knock-on effect of the legislation which made Boxing Day a public holiday in banking and commerce from the 1870s onwards. This practice was gradually taken up in industry, and the new two-day holiday gave people enough time to travel home, enjoy a brief family get-together, and travel back in time to begin work on 27 December. It is tempting to see this extension of the Christmas holiday for workers, particularly by model employers, as a piece of mid-Victorian social engineering. For decades middle-class reformers had argued that the move to the towns was tearing families apart and that city life with its great array of temptations was corrupting the younger generation. What was needed, it was said, was an annual family festival to reunite sons and daughters living away from home with their parents. Local midsummer festivals, like Wakes and Whitsun fairs, were, in the minds of reformers, too closely associated with drunkenness, vice and communal revelry to fulfil this purpose. The new middle-class family Christmas, however, had the perfect credentials: it was sentimental, child centred, and eminently respectable. *The Morning Chronicle* was an early campaigner for taking Christmas to all classes; its Christmas editorial of 1860 provides a vivid example of this kind of thinking:

On Christmas Day England gathers around the hearthstone and assembles in the family. The son separated by the cares of the world in the battle for life is reunited with his father, his mother and his sisters. But this grand opportunity of reuniting the love of families is in some danger of being lost to us. Our intense commercial life has brought with it something of a peripatetic existence to us all. Locomotion has changed the face of English society. A family that, forty years ago, would have been easily gathered together at an hour's notice, cannot now be assembled except at great inconvenience to every member, at great expense and with notice. The struggle for existence calls away boys from the roof of the parent into the crowded and busy city. The daughter too has left her mother's admonishing but tender eye. To such, a recurrence of Christmas is the only opportunity of joyful reunion. But when it is confined as a holiday of one day, the

The signalman's Christmas dinner, 1890. Many such workers continued to work on Christmas Day into our century

88

R.Taylor   A.FORESTIER 1890

opportunity is useless for the purpose of family affection. Only by an act of self denial, by closing our banks, our wharves, our warehouses and our shops can we give to those we employ and to thousands who live miles away the priceless pleasure of restoration to the family circle. It is certain that a generous is also a prudent and profitable course. The youth living in the centre of a great city surrounded by temptation and companions ready to lead him astray, may be stayed in his course by a visit to his early home.

The one-day extension of the Christmas holiday from the 1870s onwards coincided with the extension of the national railway network which in the last quarter of the nineteenth century brought many hundreds more towns and villages on to the railway map. At the same time, cheaper fares were introduced. This opening up of railway travel to the working classes, combined with a gradual improvement in their standard of living and the growing popularity of Christmas itself, probably led to a substantial increase in the numbers of working people travelling home for a short holiday.

During the last quarter of the nineteenth century an increasing number of working-class people seem to have changed their allegiance from midsummer to Christmas as the time to go home for a family reunion. Curiously, this change probably had a lot to do with the emergence of the seaside holiday. Cheap railway excursions to the coast meant that Wakes and revels were transplanted on to the beaches of Blackpool and Bournemouth. Whole towns and villages would, during a few chosen days in the summer, down tools and escape to their favourite seaside resort. There was still a very strong family and communal element in this exodus to the coast: whole neighbourhoods would go to, say, Skegness, year after year, and families would have attachments to particular boarding houses. But from this time onwards the idea of the great get-together at home was, for those separated from their families, increasingly fixed at Christmastime, especially in urban areas.

In rural areas, however, particularly those with poor railway links, Christmas continued to be eclipsed by the old tradition of family reunions and homecomings in the summer, right up until the First World War. This was true of a number of village Wakes in the North. In August 1892, for example, the *North Cheshire Herald* reported on the great summer migration home for Wakes week in the village of Mottram:

Among the hundreds drawn hither by this event there are fathers, mothers, sisters, brothers, sons, daughters, uncles, aunts and cousins of Mottram people. It is the great occasion of the gathering of the local clans. The Braddocks, the Goddards, the Rhodes and their numerous relations no more meet face to face, and this means that everybody who has been born and bred in Mottram meets face to face.

In the South the old summer revels had often turned into rather more restrained and respectable village fêtes, but these continued to overshadow Christmas as times of reunion in some areas. Gladys Withers remembers the annual fête in the Somerset village of Babcary in the 1900s:

It was always held on the last Thursday in July and it was the most important day of the year. We'd have a brass band playing and big tents up; it was bigger, I'd say, than Christmas. The schools would close down for a holiday and everyone's relatives would come from far and wide, usually by the old horse and cart. They'd stay for maybe a week and there was a big family feast.

What acted as the real brake on family get-togethers at Christmas in many villages (especially amongst poorer people) was the old problem of travelling any distance along muddy country roads in midwinter. Hannah Todd, brought up in the Durham mining village of Byers Green in the 1900s, remembers that as a child the only time of year she ever saw her relatives was during the summer:

At Christmas it was just mother, father, and us children for dinner and tea; nobody else ever came. My parents had moved from Consett – it was only twenty miles away, but that was a long way in those days – so our relatives never came for Christmas. I remember our family get-together was for a week in the summer. Father, he was the colliery blacksmith, and he knew a Mr Binks who'd hire out his pony and trap to him. There wasn't much room on it, and with seven children, mother and father would do two trips backwards and forwards to get us all there. That was the only time we'd see our grans, grandpas, aunties, cousins, everybody, and we'd have grand food for that week.

On the eve of the First World War the idea of a family gathering at Christmas had still not taken root amongst many – probably a majority – of working-class people. There was the great army of

labour who had to work on Christmas Day. There were upwards of two million people who worked through Christmas, including railway and bus company staff, policemen, postmen, nurses, gas workers, members of the armed forces, and, of course, domestic servants, who would be expected to spend the whole of Christmas week in the service of their employers.

At the same time it became fashionable, especially amongst the more daring, well-to-do young people of the jazz age, to spend Christmas abroad. Christmas visits to seaside resorts like Brighton started as early as the 1830s, but the real seeds of the 'continental Christmas' were sown a few decades later when a few aristocratic pioneers travelled to the Alps for winter sports or to the Côte d'Azur in search of the sun. By the 1890s this new craze had started to catch on amongst the better off, bored with the traditional family Christmas at home. Thomas Cook's were one of several travel agencies who offered package Christmas holidays in the Alps, Rome, and the Riviera for as little as ten guineas all inclusive. In the weeks leading up to Christmas fashionable magazines provided a showcase for many holidays abroad on offer, and one supposedly 'patriotic' option for families going away was the Christmas cruise on an ocean-going liner. In 1932 *The Lady* published an illustrated article entitled 'SPENDING CHRISTMAS IN THE SUN'. It began:

> Not long ago, it was considered not quite nice, almost unfeeling, to spend Christmas anywhere but in one's own home. But the idea of the hotel Christmas has spread (after all, for many of us it holds much greater promise of companionship and gaiety) and there are travel-lovers who long to spend Christmas in sunnier climates than ours, and under gayer skies. To the patriotic, a cruise is still the best way to a foreign holiday, and many tempting cruises have been planned for this Christmas by the steamship lines. The Asturias provide a Christmas week-end cruise for many busy people, leaving Southampton on December 23rd, spending Christmas Day in Santander, on the north coast of Spain, and reaching home on the 27th. The prices for the week-end range from 8 guineas.

For the great majority of middle-class families, however, the traditional family gathering at Christmas carried on much as it had before

Christmas at sea. Supplies of holly and mistletoe are delivered to a ship working through the festival

93

the war. Ken Reed's family were boot and shoe manufacturers in Wolverhampton in the early part of the century:

It was a convention that the whole family always went to Grandma's on Christmas Day. She lived in Tettenhall – a better class suburb, you'd call it – and there would be more than twenty of us, mother and father, aunts and uncles, and not forgetting the maid Esther from the workhouse. You'd always have to wear your Sunday best, suit and shirt and tie and that sort of thing, and you had to be on your best behaviour. We lost Uncle Sid in the Great War, but when it was over I don't remember the Christmases changing at all. It was everyone to Grandma's on Christmas Day, then everybody back to father's – he was the eldest son, you see – for Boxing Day.

For most working-class families a large family get-together like this at Christmas continued to be the exception rather than the rule throughout the inter-war years. By this time several generations of labour migration into the cities had created a patchwork of closely knit inner-city communities in which most families had many relatives living nearby. But our interviews suggest that despite this physical closeness most working-class families did not stage big Christmas get-togethers, at least not in the 'traditional' sense of a huge dinner at home with all the members of the family present. Poverty, low wages, overcrowded conditions, inadequate cooking facilities, and the many restrictions of the tiny roomed tenements and terraces where so many people lived, all combined to make any elaborate home festival a difficult or impossible proposition. For these reasons it was quite rare for the Christmas dinner to involve anyone other than the immediate family of mum, dad, and the children.

It was probably for this reason that the celebration of Christmas was so 'invisible' in the social investigations into working-class life, which began in earnest with Charles Booth's mammoth study of life and labour in London during the 1890s. If there were any big get-togethers amongst family and friends, they were much more likely to take place in the boozy atmosphere of pubs and clubs – worlds away from the middle-class Christmas at home. In some poorer areas many men seem to have spent most of Christmas Day drinking, while many women spent most of it cooking and clearing up the Christmas meal.

Victorian family reunion at Christmas. Until the late nineteenth century midwinter reunions were largely restricted to the better off

C.J. STANILAND.

The closest these communities came to the Dickensian ideal of the family reunion at Christmas was a 'high-tea' followed by an evening 'booze-up' at a chosen member of the family's home. Jim Humphries, the son of a miner, remembers these family gatherings from his childhood days in Cobridge, Stoke-on-Trent, in the 1920s:

About half past four on Christmas Day, all the family would go trooping off to Auntie Queenie's. Her house would be packed; all our relatives would be there – the same faces year after year. We'd have ham sandwiches, celery, cheese, and crisps – they were a real treat for us at the time. The living room was so small that only a couple of people could go in and get food at the same time, so we ate in shifts. Then, as the evening wore on, the beer started flowing, the women started to drink sherry, and there'd be fizzy lemonade and dandelion and burdock for the kids.

During the inter-war years entertainment seems to have sometimes been as important as family get-togethers on Christmas Day in working-class communities. Soccer, rugby league, and rugby union matches, and greyhound meetings, were all regular features of the working-class Christmas. Most of them were staged in the morning and they often recorded much higher attendances than at any other time of the year. Christmas was one of the few public holidays when everyone could enjoy some entertainment, often in the form of spectator sports. This was an era when many still had to work on Saturday afternoons and when paid holidays for all – enshrined in the 1938 Paid Holidays Act, but not implemented until after the war – were a luxury enjoyed only by a privileged minority of workers. Going to a match was probably a much more attractive proposition than staying home to talk to relatives who you probably saw most of the days of the week at work or in the street.

It was only in the post-war years that the large family gatherings at home became an established convention of the working-class Christmas. A cluster of changes combined to bring the Dickensian ideal of the homecoming within the grasp of most families for the first time since it was conceived more than a century before. 'Real' wages doubled between the early 1950s and the late 1960s providing much

Opposite: The danger of the sea is used to heighten the sentimental appeal of the Christmas family reunion in this 1879 magazine illustration

Overleaf: The Dickensian-style family gathering didn't come within the reach of most working-class families until the 1950s

more disposable income to spend on Christmas; housing conditions were substantially improved with the great public housing drive, begun in earnest after the First World War but continued even more vigorously after the Second; the average number of children born to working-class families decreased from five in the Edwardian period, to two in the post-war years, thus providing space and flexibility for Christmas family reunions; paid holidays became established and the Christmas holiday period in industry was stretched from two days to a week by the late 1960s; the number of people required to work over Christmas dropped dramatically as trade unions demanded more holidays and the era of the live-in domestic servant in the middle-class home finally came to an end; the coming of television and the scheduling of an array of the most popular programmes on Christmas Day encouraged people to spend the day at home, or at least in someone else's home; and mass car ownership made it easy to bring relatives together for Christmas and drive them home again. At the same time, the idea of family get-togethers was encouraged and exploited by industries catering for the Christmas market, who had much to gain from their promotion. By the late 1950s the home gathering had achieved such popularity that sporting fixtures were abandoned because crowds were falling off and players wanted to be with their families on Christmas Day.

The domestic family Christmas was by this time a possibility for nearly everyone, and when they had the opportunity to celebrate it they did so in a way pioneered by the well-to-do in the nineteenth century with all the trappings of the Victorian festival. We shall explore the growing popularity of these Christmas rituals in the remaining chapters.

Above: By the 1930s the railways could barely cope with the volume of passengers and goods traffic during Christmas week

Below: For many poor children, the first real Christmas they experienced was as evacuees in the Second World War. These are enjoying a party at Shenfield, Essex

Under the Christmas Tree

CHAPTER FIVE

The lighted Christmas tree was both the most spectacular and most dangerous of all the Victorian fashions for Christmas. Burning candles, perched on the dry branches of the fir trees, caused many a Christmas tragedy as whole trees went up in smoke or unlucky revellers caught alight as they brushed by the branches. From the mid nineteenth century onwards there was a race to invent a safe candleholder for the Christmas tree. One of the most bizarre inventions was a wooden ring with candle sockets every few inches which sat on the branches – this was only effective however, if the branches were flat and even. The spring clip holder, still used today, arrived from the United States in the 1880s. Though it prevented candles falling off as they had in the past, they could still slip and cause fires if undetected. One solution to this problem was to light the tree only for an hour or so, usually on Christmas Day. In the grander houses footmen would guard and patrol the lighted tree, a tradition that is just within living memory. Jack Gosney was a young footman at Sherborne Castle during the First World War:

> One of my most important jobs was to walk round the tree with a wet sponge on the top of a pole, and as the candles burnt down I used to put them out safely with the wet sponge, thereby doing away with the risk of fire. Fire was an ever-present hazard in a place like Sherborne Castle with all its valuable paintings. The staff used to come and line up in front of the tree, and Mrs Wingfield-Digby used to give each one a present and I'd wander round the tree, not paying any attention to anyone else until the whole little ceremony was finished and all the candles were out.

The fire risk was eventually solved by the coming of electricity and the production of tiny electric-powered 'fairy' lights for the Christmas tree. These were marketed in Britain from around the 1890s onwards, and were very popular in the half million or so homes that were wired

Previous pages: As a Christmas treat parents sometimes let the children choose the tree themselves. But even by the late 1920s – when this photo was taken – they were largely restricted to better off families

Opposite: The picture that started a fashion. The Christmas tree, an import from Germany, was popularized by Prince Albert who had lavishly decorated trees at Windsor from the 1840s onwards

105

up for electricity by the eve of the First World War. However, they remained a luxury for the well-to-do until after the last war.

The grim determination to possess a Christmas tree and light it, despite the risks it involved, shows how immensely important the tree was for the Victorian middle classes as the centrepiece of their home's Christmas decoration. This fascination with the lighted fir tree reaches back – consciously or unconsciously – to the pagan midwinter festivals of Saturnalia and Yuletide, in which the ritual use of fire and evergreens had acted as a kind of fertility rite to ensure the coming of spring. The Christmas tree custom (as seen in Chapter One) was an import from Germany. It arrived with the Hanoverians in the eighteenth century and became a court fashion, being popularized by Prince Albert, who adopted the practice of having a tree at Windsor from the 1840s onwards. The famous engraving in *The Illustrated London News* of 1848 showing Prince Albert, Queen Victoria, and their

Christmas was taken so seriously by Queen Victoria and Prince Albert that all their children were given their own Christmas tree, like this one pictured at Windsor in the 1860s

children, standing beside their Christmas tree probably played no small part in spreading the fashion.

In the mid 1840s newspapers actually had to explain to their readers what a Christmas tree was. Thus, *The Illustrated London News* of December 1845 describes a children's Christmas party held at the London Mission Hall:

> ... crowned by the exhibition of a German Christmas Tree or Tree of Love, which was erected upon the stage of the Hall. This is the usual mode of celebrating the Eve of the birth of Christ, in Germany and on the Continent. In almost every family is set up this pleasing figure, having the resemblance of a growing tree, loaded with a profusion of fruits and flowers; and upon its branches, the different members of the family suspend the little presents which they intend for those they love best; and on the Exhibition of the Tree, the presents are claimed by the donors, and handed, with compliments, to their friends.

By the mid 1850s the Christmas tree had firmly established itself as a middle-class Christmas convention – a rapid development for the time, and testimony to the new age of mass communications that was emerging. By December 1855 *The Lady's Newspaper* was describing 'natural fir trees' as 'very popular' and was recommending readers to try artificial trees so as to be different. In particular it recommended 'the artificial palm tree' with 'green calico leaves', which it claimed was superior to the natural fir tree because it 'tends to bring into play the ingenuity and taste of both young ladies and young gentlemen'.

The Christmas tree became so popular so quickly because it immediately fulfilled several functions in the new middle-class Christmas. It could be displayed and decorated in the home, the focal point of the Victorian family Christmas; presents could be hung from the branches, thus lending excitement to the emerging custom of present-giving at Christmas; and, most important, the idea of a decorated tree was enormously appealing to children who were increasingly becoming the focus of this Christmas festival. Indeed, most of the early accounts of Christmas trees and their decorations and presents show how they were primarily intended for the amusement of children. In 1854 a particularly evocative description of the Christmas tree by Charles Dickens appeared in *Household Words*:

> I have been looking on this evening at a merry company of children assembled around that pretty German toy, a Christmas Tree. The tree was planted in the middle of a great round table, and towered high above their heads. It was brilliantly lighted by a

The home-made palm tree with calico leaves was recommended to the upper-class readers of The Lady's Newspaper *for Christmas 1855 as one way of being different from the masses*

multitude of little tapers; and everywhere sparkled and glittered with bright objects. There were rosy cheeked dolls, hiding behind the green leaves; and there were real watches (with movable hands at least, and an endless capacity of being wound up) dangling from innumerable twigs; there were French polished tables, chairs, bedsteads, wardrobes, eight day clocks, and various other articles of domestic furniture (wonderfully made, in tin, at Wolverhampton), perched among the boughs, as if in preparation for some fairy housekeeping; there were jolly, broad faced little men, much more agreeable in appearance than many real men – and no wonder, for their heads took off, and showed them to be full of sugar plums; there were fiddles and drums . . . there were teetotums, humming tops, needle-cases, pen-wipers, smelling-bottles, conversation cards, bouquet-holders, real fruit, made artificially dazzling with goldleaf; imitation apples, pears and walnuts, crammed with surprise; in short, as a pretty child, before me, delightedly whispered to another pretty child, her bosom friend, 'There was everything, and more.'

Although the Christmas tree rapidly took root as an essential part of the Christmas festival, it was not until the 1880s that Christmas Day was finally fixed as the day when it was to be lit up in all its glory and the presents on it distributed. Up to that point, the old Twelfth Night tradition had tugged it towards 6 January, especially in rural backwaters where old customs died hard. The Rev. Francis Kilvert, for example, describing a rural parish in Wiltshire, wrote in his diary on 7 January 1873 that 'there had been a Christmas Party with a Christmas tree at 5 o'clock'.

While the Christmas tree quickly established itself as the centrepiece of the middle-class living room, the walls and ceilings would be lavishly decked with evergreens. These Christmas decorations were nothing new, but in late Victorian years they became almost a high art in well-to-do homes, with ladies' magazines giving lengthy instructions on how to furnish rooms tastefully for Christmas with holly, mistletoe, and ivy. Twigs and branches would be carefully arranged around windows, fireplaces, and paintings, or suspended from the ceiling. These decorations would be interspersed everywhere with huge, hanging mottos, the most popular of which read 'A Hundred Thousand Welcomes', 'Pray You Walk In', and 'A Happy Christmas'. These mottos were often made from tiny everlasting flowers, cotton wool, or tinfoil, and would be lavishly bordered with moss or mixed evergreens. Christmas issues of ladies' journals were most emphatic in their demand that Christmas decorations be taken very seriously; they

The Christmas tree in Victorian and Edwardian times was essentially for the children, as this stereograph suggests

were probably quite influential in making them an important feature of the Victorian middle-class Christmas. Not only were women — assisted by their children and servants – expected to begin making and arranging these decorations weeks before Christmas, they were also encouraged to observe rules governing every last detail, even down to the decoration of the Christmas table. In December 1896, for example, *The Lady* reprimanded its readers for the 'much-to-be-regretted fact that many hostesses who at other seasons of the year pride themselves on the dainty appointments of their dinner table rest content with a meagre decoration of a few stiff, tastelessly arranged sprigs of evergreens, a couple of pots of ferns, or at most a solitary vase of white chrysanthemums or Christmas roses, minus any vestige of foliage'. To liven things up *The Lady* recommended:

A decidedly novel notion for the adornment of a Christmas dinner or supper table. Down the centre of the table runs a long narrow slip of looking glass, bordered all round with a bank of feathery moss, holly, mistletoe and sprays of red-veined tree ivy, in which some electric lamps, or, failing these, fairy lights are half hid. At each corner a miniature Christmas tree – in reality the top of a seedling fir gleaming with frostine powder, is fixed. The mimic lake is studded with islands of greenery, from which rise other little trees, and here and there are placed birch-bark canoes, painted with silver paint, and each apparently guided by a 'Father Christmas', bright with silvery drapery, the boats being freighted with glittering white bon-bons. The effect of the whole is very striking and quaint.

The growing demand for Christmas trees and decorations helped to create a thriving evergreen economy in the late Victorian years. The only source of information we have discovered on the Christmas tree economy is an article entitled 'THE CHRISTMAS TREE VENDOR' which appeared in *The English Illustrated Magazine* in December 1895. It takes the form of a conversation with a man who is described as being 'the high priest of the Christmas tree trade' at Covent Garden market in London. His company was the largest supplier of Christmas trees in Britain, and in the capital his family had dominated the trade since the 1830s.

'We deal in trees of every description,' he said, 'from the spruce fir, forty feet high, to the tiny slip of eighteen inches – a mere toy of a thing, that people who have one child buy to amuse it.'
  'How many do you sell?'
  'Well, about thirty thousand of all sizes every year.'

'A huge forest. Where do they come from – abroad?'

'Why no, the greater number we get from Yorkshire. The trees come from gentlemen's game reserves – they are thinnings; when the tops get too high, out the tree has to come. We get nursery-men's thinnings as well for the little eighteen inch slips. . . .'

'What do we get for them? Well, all prices. A forty-foot tree runs to about six pounds or thereby; a twenty-foot one about four pounds; and so on down to the smallest.'

'Which sells at?'

'Fourpence, cheap enough surely. . . .'

'How many forty-foot trees would you dispose of?'

'Usually about a hundred. They go chiefly to public institu-tions. The Crystal Palace people always require some of the biggest.'

'And the great shopkeepers?'

'Well, they usually go in for about twenty feet high or so. In the matter of charitable institutions there's a good deal of busi-ness. . . . It's very interesting when I'm fitting up the tree in the ward of a children's hospital to see the excitement. We do it at night, and the little things are almost wild with delight. They ought to be asleep, of course; but they get wind of what's going on and can hardly be kept in bed. It's funny to see all the eager little faces stretching up to catch a glimpse of the show beforehand.'

'You have lots of little customers, I suppose, who were able to come here?'

'Oh yes. If the last fortnight of November is fine (that's the briskest business time) when all the trees are on hand, we've had any number of children at the Market. They're brought down to pick and choose their own tree. Lots of them are from the West End. . . .'

'From the middle of October,' my forester continued, 'or even earlier, we begin taking orders. We supply the trade very exten-sively.'

'And the barrow men?'

'Yes, but these hawkers deal only in the very smallest and cheapest kinds. . . .'

In late Victorian and Edwardian times, poor families would be much more likely to put up Christmas decorations than a Christmas tree. Because evergreens could be collected from woods and hedge-rows for free, the centuries-old tradition of decorating homes with them continued throughout the nineteenth century. Some local cus-toms of decoration reached back to pagan times. For example, in

Collecting mistletoe and holly for decorating houses is a centuries-old tradition

December 1893 *The Lady* had an article on surviving folk customs, including the report that 'our West Country girls have a pretty custom of trimming their beds with holly on Christmas Eve. They say the evil spirits will harm them if they omit this Christmas ceremony.' If contemporary illustrations are anything to go by, it was common practice for children to chop down and collect holly and mistletoe and carry it home. One popular poor man's decoration was 'the kissing bough', which in the North was often called a 'mistletoe'. It consisted of a decorated object, like apple barrel hoops clamped together, from which oranges, apples, tinsel, sugar mice, and so on, would dangle down on a string. Alf Todd remembers the tradition of making the mistletoes in the Northumberland village of Byers Green in the early part of the century:

> In every home in the North you found a mistletoe when I was young. Now to make a mistletoe what you used to do was to take the hoops off the barrel (as you know all the apples come in a

The Christmas holly cart in a London suburb, 1848. The seasonal trade gave a much needed boost to the poor street trader

barrel). Then we used to buy coloured tissue paper, cut it in strips, and wrap it round the hoops. Then after we'd done that, we'd hang little toys – bits of tinsel, baubles, anything we could – from it, and put the whole thing hanging from the ceiling. This was one of the main features of the house at Christmas.

While middle-class families had carefully designed mottos hanging around rooms, poor families had to make do with a much more rough and ready seasonal message. Rose Ashton, recalling her childhood in Barrow at the turn of the century, remembers, 'at Christmastime, before we went to bed, dad used to write all around the hearth, "A Happy Christmas To You" in white chalk'. In the towns and cities home-made paper chains, usually stuck together with flour paste by children a few days before Christmas, were the most common decoration in working-class homes from the 1850s onwards. But 'street-wise' children like Ted Harrison, brought up in London's East End in the 1900s, often managed to put on quite a good display of decorations:

A couple of days before Christmas I used to go round De Beauvoir Park. That's where the rich people lived, and they had gardens and we used to pinch the laurel branches. I wouldn't try the old holly – it was too bleedin' prickly – so my brother brought the holly. You'd decorate the room with that, hang 'em around a picture of Uncle Jo. And we used to make artificial flowers so we didn't take some back to the shop. We always managed to keep a few and decorate me grannie's bonnet. And we made a wreath, and hung it on the door knocker just to show how posh we were.

This same family put up ingenious home-made fairy lights to light up and decorate the back yard for the drinking sessions they had on Christmas Eve and Christmas night:

Just before Christmas we'd have to wash the fairy lights – they were glass jars, all different colours. They had what they called a farthing candle, a small candle in them, and they were put out in the yard to light the way to the toilet on Christmas Eve and Christmas night. The toilet was at the end of the garden, you see, and when the people went out they couldn't see the way in the bleedin' dark, so they used to have these fairy lights for light to get up to the kahsi [toilet].

Although they made makeshift decorations, most working-class families would not have had a Christmas tree. Fir tree cuttings from landed estates were hard to come by in the countryside, and had to be bought in the city. To spend a shilling or so on a fir tree, only to throw it away a few weeks later, was seen by most working families as an extravagant luxury. But rural families were able to improvise their own substitute Christmas trees. Alf Todd remembers the old Northumberland tradition of decorating holly bushes in the style of the Christmas tree:

We didn't have Christmas trees up here in Northumberland. I don't know if they were too poor or what, but we didn't have Christmas trees, so you used to try and find a nice holly tree out in the wood. And you used to keep your eye on that holly tree and, when it came time, before Christmas, if you were lucky enough you were able to cut it. But if somebody beat you, well, you didn't get one. Then what we used to do, we used to decorate it, put streamers down, make it lifelike, and we'd hang all these little toys until you got your tree absolutely covered. And then at night you used to put it in the window where people could see it. And it was a grand thing for people to come in and see who had the best tree; it was like a competition.

The first contact that millions of poorer people had with the ritual of present giving from the Christmas tree was on entering domestic service. It was a common practice in most households for the staff to be given a present from the tree. It was probably no coincidence that the Christmas tree, which began essentially as a children's toy, should start to be used for the servants – for children and servants, both of whom were 'dependent beings' with few rights, would have been closely connected in the mind of the head of the house. In larger houses and on country estates, the present giving often took the form of a grand Christmas Day ritual. Charles De'ath began work at Hallingbury Place in Essex around the time of the First World War:

How well I remember the Christmases at Hallingbury Place, a massive country house. They used to have all the villagers, the men who worked on the estate, all fourteen gardeners, grooms, and laundry people (they had their own laundry) all around the Christmas tree. I can see the old gardener now. They used to drag the tree in, and it used to go right up to the top of the ceiling in this massive old servants' hall. The room was packed. I stood and watched the whole procedure. They were really happy these people; it was pleasant to see them enjoying themselves. Mrs

Overleaf: The Christmas tree became so popular so quickly because it fitted the increasing preoccupation with family-based entertainments at Christmas. This picture was taken in London, Christmas 1919

Taking home the Christmas tree in Cheshire, 1935

Agnew and the lady's maid used to give the presents to everyone and to all the children who worked on the estate. I remember she turned round to the lady's maid, and she said, 'Oh, we mustn't forget the little fat boy.' I was the hall boy, and I was as fat as a little pudding when I was about fifteen. And I remember quite clearly she gave me a pair of socks, off the Christmas tree. And I think everybody went home happy.

In many homes the servants would be asked beforehand what they wanted to receive in the present giving ritual. Jack Gosney recalls:

It was the custom for the housekeeper to ask all the servants – perhaps a dozen or more – what they would like for Christmas, then report to the Lady of the house, Mrs Wingfield-Digby. On Christmas Day they'd all line up and she'd present them with the presents from beneath the tree. The outside staff had a couple of rabbits; perhaps the heads had a pheasant. The presents for the inside staff always took the form of something useful. I have a strong tin trunk which was such a present way back in 1917, and my first one was a pink shirt.

By the time of the Great War a Christmas tree in the home was still quite a rarity in working-class families, and the custom was nowhere near so universal as it was in Germany. It is quite likely that for some British soldiers their first glimpse of a Christmas tree was the eerie sight of thousands with their candles flickering above the German trenches on the Western Front in Christmas 1914 (see page 27).

There was little change in the class distinction in Christmas decorations during the inter-war years. Many poor people still couldn't afford Christmas trees, though some did buy cheap artificial trees which could be used year after year. Izal, the makers of toilet equipment, began manufacturing them after the war, and the early prototypes in fact looked a little like toilet brushes. It was really only from the mid 1950s onwards that Christmas trees, decorations, and cards became big business as most working-class families had money to spare at the festive season for the first time. By the late 1970s Christmas decorations had become a multi-million pound industry, which in time produced electric decorations, some of them for municipal displays, the most spectacular of which was Regent Street in London.

The growing conformity to the kind of celebration which began in the nineteenth century was reflected, too, in what people cooked and ate at Christmas – as will be seen in the next chapter.

Christmas Fare

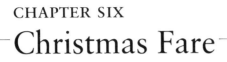

CHAPTER SIX

A Victorian cookery correspondent, mulling over the proper fare for a Christmas feast, remarked that if you had a plum pudding, turkey and all the trimmings in August, it would still be Christmas dinner. It is a bit like the Greek philosopher Aristotle's puzzle over breakfast: is it what you eat, or the time that you eat it that is important? Nowadays, with battery reared turkeys and packaged plum puddings, it is in fact possible to knock out a Christmas dinner any time you like. Attempts are made to shift a surplus of frozen turkeys at Easter. The revolution in farming and eating habits has caused some confusion about the proper fare for Christmas, and, historically, this has probably been the least fixed of the rituals attached to the modern festival. However, there remains a fairly well-defined idea of what you *ought* to have for Christmas, with turkey still top of the list; other essentials are Christmas or plum pudding, and a Christmas cake.

In many ways, the evolution of the classic Christmas dinner followed the course of the creation of other rituals associated with the modern festival: it was middle class; it absorbed ingredients formerly associated with other feast days in the seasonal calendar; it became less varied as the celebrations gained national acceptance; it was well beyond the means of a large section of the population until the 1950s or 1960s. As a consequence, it was available to the fortunate few, and, among the poor, mostly available only out of a charitable hamper. One example of this is seen in *A Christmas Carol*, where Dickens makes Scrooge, to mark his conversion to the new Christmas spirit, send a turkey round to the family of his poor clerk, Bob Cratchit.

The story of the turkey itself is an interesting one. Like many domesticated farm animals, the turkey is not native to Britain. It was first brought to England, and other parts of Europe, in the middle of the sixteenth century from central and western America, where it was both a domesticated bird and one hunted in the wild woods of Alabama. (It probably got the name turkey because its strange head resembled the head-dress of Turkish men.) At the time the turkey was introduced, the mute swan was the most prized bird for great feasts. But swans were difficult to rear – they bred in the wild and were rounded up each year in July at the 'uppings' and the cygnets taken to

Previous pages: A Christmas tea in 1900. At that time only the privileged few would eat chicken or turkey on Christmas Day

Between the wars, turkeys were often sold alive and kicking – they were a delicacy before the days of battery farming

swan pits to be fattened for the table. From the moment it arrived in Britain, the turkey was successful as a domesticated bird, and swans declined in importance as food for feasts.

Although the turkey became associated with Christmas dinner quite early on, it was just one of a mass of feathered creatures which were slain for great banquets. It was not specifically a Christmas dish, unlike boar's head for example (the boar having been a sacred animal among Nordic peoples and its sacrifice a religious ritual).

By the late eighteenth century, however, the turkey was becoming *the* fashionable Christmas bird for the well-to-do in London; and when the modern festival began to take shape in the early 1800s, it was readily available as an alternative to goose or roast beef. Turkeys were reared in Cambridgeshire and Norfolk, and driven to London from August onwards with small leather boots on their feet, or a coating of tar as protective wear for the journey. During the nineteenth century more and more were slaughtered at the farm and taken by stagecoach from Norwich to London (a three-day journey).

William Hervey, an early folklorist, describes the scene in the 1830s:

Many a time we have seen a Norfolk coach with its hampers piled on the roof and swung from beneath the body, and its birds depending, by every possible contrivance, from every part from which a bird could be made to hang. Nay, we believe it is not unusual with the proprietors, at this season, to refuse inside passengers of the human species in favour of these oriental gentry who 'pay better'.

There is no contemporary evidence which explains why the turkey became especially associated with Christmas, but it is fair to assume that as the largest bird available – weighing anything up to 40 lbs – it suited very well the size of family Christmas gatherings of the middle classes, which probably averaged from fourteen to twenty people. Whereas the feasts of the rural gentry had included a mass of different foods, the more restrained dinner of the middle-class Victorians could have one large turkey as its centrepiece.

Turkey breeders in time produced smaller birds to satisfy a growing market of smaller families. Between the two world wars, the average size of the birds went down markedly, as *Picture Post* noted in 1938: 'Up to about 12 years ago a 20 lb turkey was the standard family size. Now in these days of smaller families and flats, people do not want birds bigger than 12 or 16 lbs.'

In the same report, there is mention of 'slate clubs' to which poorer people contributed, often from one Christmas to the next: 'The shilling a week Slate Clubs are the backbone of the turkey trade among poor people. Ten shillings is usually allotted for a turkey or a joint, and if ten shillings won't buy a turkey, so much the worse for the poulterers . . . If prices rise many people use their slate club money which would otherwise have bought a turkey, for something cheaper.'

One of the problems with this over-sized bird was that, even if poorer people could afford it, they did not have a large enough oven in which to cook it. The turkey which would not fit in the cooker was a standard joke after the Second World War, and the kitchen facilities available to poor people were often primitive or non-existent.

The turkey did not become widely available at the right price and the right size until the years of battery farming, better housing and post-war affluence, and by that time it had lost its ritual significance through over-production. Yet, long before then, poorer people had made an effort to get together some kind of Christmas dinner which marked it out as a special occasion.

A splendid illustration of the hierarchy of Christmas dinner in the 1930s – rabbit was as common as turkey

S.T. DADD.

R. TAYLOR.

In the nineteenth century, it was the goose club which was the most important institution for the artisans, particularly those of southern England – in the North, beef remained a more common centrepiece for the Christmas dinner. Goose clubs became very popular after the railways were built in the 1840s, for geese were cheaper (they were a tougher meat) than turkeys and could be transported *en masse* to the cities, London in particular. Very often the clubs were organized in pubs, and workmen would pay in for several months in the hope of winning a bird in a raffle just before Christmas. Christmas clubs are still quite common, of course, but in that period getting any kind of special Christmas dinner was much more of a gamble. Most people would get something for their contributions, but the clubs were a kind of lottery in which some did much better than others. Bottles of whisky and port were often raffled with the goose. The association of goose clubs with drinking gave them a bad name in the Temperance Movement, which argued that they did more harm than good. *The Illustrated London News* of 1852 reflected this concern:

These clubs are got up for the 'benefit of the house' as it is called; and there is but little doubt that, with the money spent over the meetings, every goose costs at least a pound in the end. . . . A perfect babble of sound is a public-house on Christmas Eve when the prizes are drawn, and many a pint of gin is won and lost about the weight of the different geese before the members separate for the night.

To ensure that no cheating went on, the draw was often performed by a child, observed by disinterested elderly gentlemen. But the winners of this Christmas gamble very often carried off a bird which was so large they could not cook it at home. Instead they would take it to the local bakers, who kept their ovens going over Christmas, and on Christmas morning they would dress in their best clothes and carry the steaming meal back through the streets. A very snooty description of this is given in *The Illustrated London News* of 1848:

It is not every day in the week or year that the poor can dine; and however vulgar may be the snob that arrays himself in his best on Christmas Day and brings home his dinner steaming hot from the convenient shop of Rusk the baker, it would be both churlish and

A child, as in this illustration, often made the Christmas draw in the Goose Club to ensure fair play

Taking home the Christmas dinner cooked in the baker's oven. This is the 1840s, but the custom survived until the 1920s

snobbish of us, or anyone else, to look with unsympathetic eyes, or turn up our noses contemptuously upon the harmless and well-won enjoyment that is expressed upon his countenance.

In the countryside it was common for cottagers to take their Christmas dinners to the local bakers – but only the baker and his family was able to afford goose. Gladys Withers can recall Christmas before 1914, when her father was the village baker in Babcary, Somerset:

We always had a big fat goose. My father would be at the head of the table, and the children would sit still until the youngest one said grace, very, very quietly, then operations would begin. My father only stopped baking on Christmas Day and Boxing Day, but he had to keep the ovens going (these were wood fired) otherwise it would take such a long time to get the heat up afterwards. The cottagers would bring in their Christmas dinners, and what an array there would be! Rabbits with their heads pinned back so they would be sitting up on a meat tin; pigeons all nicely trussed up. But I suppose the greatest delicacy would be blackbird pie, only the breasts and legs were used, and the feet were cleaned and would protrude in a little bunch through the pastry.

Rabbit was quite common Christmas fare in these rural areas, and it was possible for cottagers to get most of what they needed for Christmas from the hedgerows and fields around. Blackbirds were caught at night by trapping them in a large net into which they flew when frightened by a wooden bat – hence the term 'bird-batting'.

In London, and other large cities, it was quite common for poorer people to keep poultry in their back yard, and to sell the few eggs they could for extra income. The cockerel was not, as a rule, fattened up for Christmas dinner, but Ted Harrison from London recalls the time they did themselves proud:

My mother used to keep fowls and she had this big cockerel. She called it Wild Bill Hickock, but I called it Billy the Sod because it would go for you when you went to the toilet in the back yard. My sister got locked in the toilet once because she was scared of him, and my mother had to hunch the bird away. Well, that signed his death warrant. My mother slung her apron over his head and wrung his neck and we had him for Christmas dinner. Normally mother used to buy a pig's head because they were cheap, and just before she brought it into the kitchen she'd force an apple into its mouth.

Ted Harrison also remembers what a time-consuming thing it was to prepare the Christmas pudding, in their cramped house with only a wood burning fire. It took several days to cook the pudding, and as a child he had the responsibility of watching the fire so that it did not go out:

You couldn't get stoned raisins then, so us kids used to have to sit round in the evening and stone the raisins for the pudding. Then I used to have to go to the local sawmills and get loads of chips and I had to sit three days before Christmas out by the copper, where you used to boil the clothes. And we used it for the pudding and I was all day shovelling these bleeding chips in the fire – mustn't let it go off the boil. We put in black beer, and grated carrots, and apples.

A fine display of poultry and meat in Manchester in 1900, with a pig's head amongst the corpses. For many families Christmas was the only time they would eat chicken

This same family also kept up the tradition described in Dickens' *Sketches by Boz* of all the family having a stir at the Christmas pudding. As you stirred you made a wish. Coins were also put in the pudding, so that it contained magic charms, and eating it was a game of chance.

The origins of this part of the Christmas ritual are rather obscure. Christmas or mince pies, containing a mix of sweet and savoury ingredients, had been made for hundreds of years (Elizabethan cookery contained a great many spices). In the modern Christmas, mince pies, plum pudding, and Christmas cake are all regarded as 'traditional'. There is a confusion about their relative significance; they all appear to be related to the same impulse not only to create a special kind of feast, but to introduce into the baking and eating a game of chance and telling of fortunes for the coming year.

In the nineteenth century, though plum puddings were eaten on Christmas Day, the baking of cakes was much more associated with Twelfth Night. In 1840, Leigh Hunt wrote: 'Christmas goes out in fine style – with Twelfth Night. It is a finish worthy of the time. Christmas Day was the morning of the season: New Year's Day the middle of it, or noon; Twelfth Night is the night, brilliant with innumerable planets of Twelfth Cakes.'

The Twelfth cake was more like a modern wedding cake in appearance than the Christmas cakes we have now with robins, snow, and winter scenes. The largest Twelfth cakes were made by confectioners for window displays: in 1811 there was one advertised by a shop in London's Cheapside which reputedly weighed half a ton. In the 1840s and 1850s, *The Illustrated London News* gave descriptions of the more splendid constructions, including this one of Queen Victoria's Twelfth cake for 1849:

> The cake was of regal dimensions, being about 30 inches in diameter, and tall in proportion: round the side the decorations consisted of strips of gilded paper, bowing outwards near the top, issuing from an elegant gold bordering. The figures, of which there were 16, on top of the cake, represented a part of beaux and belles of the last century enjoying a repast *al fresco* under some trees . . .

At this time the popularity of Twelfth cakes was at a peak but by the 1870s they seem to have more or less disappeared, and references are made to smaller cakes eaten on Christmas Day. Families did buy Twelfth cakes to take home in the 1840s and 50s, but the ritual of the really large cake appears to date from quite a different era in the history of Christmas when the event was more of a community and less of a family affair. Up to the eighteenth century, the custom with Twelfth cakes was to hide a bean and a pea in the raw cake mixture. When it was baked the man with the bean was elected King, and the woman with the pea Queen. This seems to have derived from older customs in which, for a brief period of the Christmas season, anybody might be given power to oversee the festivities – a playing with fate that has always been common in midwinter revelries.

As with so many other aspects of the modern Christmas ritual, the dinner evolved in the nineteenth century into a family affair which borrowed rituals from other feast days and remodelled them into a shorter festival. But there were elements in the new festival which were entirely novel.

This extraordinary edifice was Queen Victoria's Twelfth Night cake in 1849. From these mountainous confections, the Christmas cake evolved

The Gifts of Santa Claus

CHAPTER SEVEN

Of all the new rituals associated with the Victorian revival of Christmas, the last to arrive was easily the most influential – the red-robed benevolent figure of Santa Claus. In his modern guise, he was quite unknown in Britain before the 1870s, yet by the 1890s he was appearing all over the place as people dressed up as Santa to distribute goods and excite children. The speed and enthusiasm with which his legend was greeted suggests that in some mysterious way the modern Christmas needed it. It was an embodiment of the new spirit of the season.

Santa Claus is also known as Father Christmas, which causes some historical confusion for there *was* a Father Christmas figure before the 1870s. He was a regular character in the Mummers plays performed in villages, usually with some rather drab lines like: 'Here come I, Old Father Christmas. . . .' But this figure bore little resemblance to Santa Claus. He had no fixed image; no reindeer, no sleigh, no sack of toys; and he did not come down chimneys and fill children's stockings on Christmas Eve. He represented merely a general spirit of revelry and festivity. The new Father Christmas was quite different; much more appropriate to the Victorian middle-class concern with the family, home, children, and charity. Collectively, the well-to-do *were*, in a sense, Father Christmas, because it was they who distributed what bounty there was. But they did not invent him: he arrived in Britain by a circuitous route appropriate to such a seasoned traveller, via Turkey, Holland, and America.

St Nicholas was a real-life bishop in Myra, Turkey, in the fifth century, who became the patron saint of children. In European legend, he subsequently turned up in various guises at various dates around Christmas, but particularly on 5 December, the Eve of his Saint's Day. In Dutch legend – still very much alive in Holland – St Nicholas (Sinter Klaas) was a very important figure who arrived on a white horse with his servant Black Pete, and came down chimneys to fill the shoes of good children with presents, and to leave a birch rod for those who had been bad.

This, along with many similar legends, was taken to New York (formerly New Amsterdam) in the seventeenth century where it

Previous pages: Santa Claus visits bargees and their children in Brentford, Middlesex, in 1937

Artists like the American Thomas Beale, who painted magic lantern slides in the 1880s, created the image of Santa Claus that is familiar today

remained in a *pot pourri* of folk customs which differed only in the timing of St Nick's arrival and his means of transport – either a white horse or a wagon. In the early nineteenth century, the Dutch legend became the dominant one; and in New York slang St Nicholas became 'Santiclaus'. He lost his black servant, and his time of arrival shifted to Christmas Eve. He was fêted by poets and writers, including Washington Irving who wrote about St Nick in his *Knickerbockers's History of New York* in 1809.

Until the 1820s, there was no mention of reindeer or sleighs, and there is no record in European legend of such a means of transport. It is something of a mystery how this idea caught on, and why subsequently Santa was supposed to come from the North Pole. It may all have to do with a very influential poem, 'The Night Before Christmas', written in 1822 allegedly by a theologian, Clement Clarke Moore, for the amusement of his children. He recorded and embellished contemporary accounts of Santa Claus, and fixed forever in the imagination of Americans, and in time the British, the picture of a sleigh drawn by 'eight tiny reindeer' – Dasher, Dancer, Prancer, Vixen, Comet, Cupid, Donder, and Blixen. This was sheer invention, but it had a mythical power. Interestingly, in the poem, St Nick was a 'right jolly elf', as he was in Norwegian legend, which might explain why he was able to get down chimneys.

The legend rapidly spread across America, where the modern, family Christmas was developing very much in the way it was in England – Charles Dickens' *A Christmas Carol* was a bestseller there too. Santiclaus, or Santeclaus, or St Nick, appeared on cards produced in the 1870s, and no doubt these, as well as other accounts of the man dressed in the red bishop's robes, were sent to Britain.

There was no great fanfare for Santa's arrival; rather he seems to have crept in as a new folk custom before he was publicly acknowledged. The following is an observation from the Folklore Society in 1879 on the strange custom which existed in Worcestershire and Herefordshire:

> On Christmas Eve, when the inmates of a house in the country retire to bed, all those desirous of a present place a stocking outside the door of their bedroom, with the expectation that some mythical being called *Santiclaus* will fill the stocking or place something within it before the morning. . . . An Exeter resident tells me this custom prevails also in Devonshire.

Folklorists at that time suggested that this practice had come from various European countries. None appeared to be aware that America was the true source. Santa Claus arrived here silently and darkly, then emerged as a familiar figure without people having any proper understanding of his origins. It must therefore have been what he represented, the underlying desire that he fulfilled, that made him so popular.

There have been a number of explanations for the rise of the popularity of Santa Claus in America. Because he was familiar in a number of strands of European legend, he served as a figure who integrated society; belief in him became a belief in a dominant, national culture, for Jews as well as Christians; he arose in a new consumerist age as a symbol of unlimited bounty; and he represented

It was charity which introduced the poor to the new image of Father Christmas

STRANGERS.

Father Christmas. "WHAT! NOT KNOW *ME!*—OH, THIS MUST BE ALTERED!"

CHRISTMAS SUPPLEMENT

CHRISTMAS FOR EVER!

We have seen good old customs abolished,
    To our anger, vexation, and grief;
May we ne'er grow so dainty and polished
    As at Christmas to fall from roast beef.
Nor be driven, by dandified sneering,
    Unessential plum pudding to deem,
And to look on its smoke disappearing
    From the board, as improvement in steam.

From adorning our houses with holly
    Let us never be scared by the goose
Who says 'tis an old-fashioned folly,
    And wants to know what is its use?
Let the mistletoe, too, be suspended
    Over lasses and lads as of yore,
And with blind-man's-buff Christmas attended,
    Whoever may vote it a bore.

Let a log' be consumed in all houses,
    Notwithstanding there's plenty of coal;
And 'twere jolly, at Christmas carouses,
    If roast crabs still could hiss in the bowl.

the essentially unrealistic expectations of an economy which was perpetually expanding. In particular, he became symbolic of what children demanded of parents.

The appeal of the new Father Christmas was possibly a reflection of a changing attitude towards children and childhood in this period. From the middle of the nineteenth century, there was a concern among middle-class families to make childhood and early adolescence a kind of 'quarantine' period before adulthood – to protect the young from what they saw as the bad influence of growing up too soon. It had been quite common in England for the children of the upper classes to be put with the servants in big houses until they came of age – lowly adults and unfledged gentry were temporarily on the same social footing. The development of the public schools represented a great change in attitudes, and then, from the 1870s on, this was translated into a national view with the development of the Education Acts which first made schooling compulsory. In other words, childhood became marked out as a distinct and definable period in life in which individuals were to be protected from adult responsibility – child labour was done away with.

In Britain, there was no recognition of St Nicholas's Day (6 December) in the early nineteenth century, but there were rituals in which children attempted to extract goods from adults. Foremost amongst these was Hallowe'en, the Eve of All Hallows Day (1 November) when village children would beg for food. The French anthropologist Claude Lévi-Strauss makes the point that in all societies there are rituals in which 'outsiders' – the young, the sick, and the poor – are 'worshipped' in an annual ceremony. In his rather obscure terms, the 'outsider' represents the 'dead' – those not really belonging to society proper. In essence, the Santa Claus ritual is an example – and a very widespread and powerful one – of sacrifice and appeasement.

In Victorian society, with an ever-widening gap between the social classes, it is easy to understand the great appeal of the selfless, gift-giver figure. As in the role reversal and 'topsy-turvy' associated with the season, Father Christmas or Santa Claus is the mythical distributor of goods who closes the economic divide in society. He represents a fiction that everyone in society is equal. Once Santa Claus had captured the imagination of British people he was quickly personified by the charitable middle classes. In the 1890s well-meaning ladies in London were dressing up as Santa Claus to distribute a bit of charitable Christmas cheer to the poor. A Miss F. Waggett, who joined

Old Father Christmas represented the spirit of revelry, but unlike Santa Claus did not bring gifts for children

The "Santa Claus" Gazette.

The Official Organ of the "Santa Claus" Christmas Distribution Fund.
155, ALDBOROUGH ROAD, SEVEN KINGS, ILFORD.

President: H.R.H. PRINCESS CHRISTIAN.   Vice-President: THE LADY ST. HELIER.

FOUNDED 1894.   Founder and Hon. Sec., WALTER H. STEVENS.

No. 9. VOL. 2.   1911.   ONE PENNY.

This Number contains the Report of the SEVENTEENTH Annual Distribution of CLOTHING, Dolls, Toys, &c., to 9,708 POOR CHILDREN.

This Institution has been Honoured by the approval of Her Majesty THE QUEEN also Her Majesty QUEEN ALEXANDRA who have recently contributed to its Funds

Mabel Taylor

An Appeal is now made or behalf of Ten Thousand Poor Children

The object of the Fund is to provide Parcels of Warm Clothing, Toys, etc., for Poor Children who would not, under any ordinary circumstances, participate in the joys and festivities of Christmas-tide.

Each Child receives a separate Parcel, and each Parcel is labelled and ADDRESSED TO THE CHILD and delivered at the home on Christmas Eve—*with love from " Santa Claus."*

EACH PARCEL CONTAINS—One Garment or useful article of clothing; one Toy or Doll; a Bag or Box of Sweets; and a Christmas Card.

Since the foundation of this Fund, in December, 1894, no less than

85,392 PARCELS OF WARM CLOTHING, TOYS, etc. **£8,000**
HAVE BEEN DISTRIBUTED VALUED AT UPWARDS OF

WILL YOU PLEASE HELP FOR THE COMING CHRISTMAS?

Santa Claus was a charitable figure before he became the great commercial symbol of Christmas

the Santa Claus Distribution Fund, wrote in 1897 of her escapades in London's East End: 'December 4th found us trying to assume the garb of Mrs Santa Claus, bedecking ourselves in large light wool shawls as an outer covering which enabled us in a measure to deceive the small Whitechapelites causing much exclamations, and much merriment as we wended our way through the streets and courts of Whitechapel and St George's.' The fund had formed in Stoke Newington, north-east London, in 1894 to give presents and clothing to poor children because, according to the *Santa Claus Gazette*, 'many of these hear a good deal about old "Santa Claus" coming to fill the stockings on Christmas Eve and some are tempted to hang up the stockings in a prominent place, only to find that in the morning the stockings are empty and to them, at least, the story of Santa is but a mockery. . . .'

The Santa Claus Workers' League of the Distribution Fund usually dressed up on Christmas Eve and visited poor families with parcels of clothing and toys. In 1897 these charitable lady Santas gave away 5,000 presents, including 720 pairs of warm socks and stockings, 265 scarves, 485 dolls, 90 humming tops, 55 tin trumpets, and 24 toy engines. By 1910, they were distributing 10,000 parcels at Christmas. Accounts of the wonder with which the poor greeted these visitors were given in the *Santa Claus Gazette* in 1896:

A man with six or seven children opened the door to us and when the little parcels were placed in his hands, with an explanation, he looked at us with astonishment and said he was indeed thankful as his children would have nothing, he having been out of employment for a long time. There was nothing in the house and he had not any money to purchase another meal.

There never were, of course, enough charitable Santas to keep the poor happy at Christmas, and for many years the Father Christmas myth brought as much heartache for parents and children as it did starry-eyed wonderment. Santa was supposed to reward good children and punish the bad, but the true judgement on Christmas Eve was a harsh economic one, and many parents were confronted on the following morning by their children's innocent despair. Dolly Cattle, whose father drove a brewer's dray in London, remembers this from her Islington childhood in the 1930s.

Father Christmas, we really believed in him, you know. As we stirred the Christmas pudding, we put in farthings wrapped in silver paper, and my mother used to say: 'What would you like for Christmas?' This particular year I wanted a doll and pram and she

said: 'Well, you may not be able to have both . . . Father Christmas will do what he can.' We opened our stockings and got about four new pennies, a few nuts, and a tangerine and an apple, a comic, a magic painting book, and this rag doll was perched on top – I was pleased with it, you know, until we went out to play, and my friend came out with this beautiful twin pram and twin dolls. I said: 'Father Christmas is not very fair, Mum, is he?' Her eyes filled with tears, and she said there wasn't a Father Christmas, it was just make-believe, and Mum and Dad bought the presents, and they couldn't afford any more.

Poor parents could be quite ingenious – as no doubt they still are – in tackling the inevitable gap between their child's expectations and what they could afford. Betty Ward's mother had no money and four children to please:

We came to Jarrow in 1926. My father was a farm labourer and he wasn't entitled to any benefits. There was no money, so my mother used to tell us, 'Don't be disappointed if Father Christmas doesn't leave you anything. He'll probably leave you a letter and you'll get what he says in it!' So on Christmas morning there'd be the stocking with fruit and nuts and a halfpenny, and then a letter from Father Christmas, which we later discovered was written by my father and it would say that either he hadn't got what we wanted or hadn't time to go back, but rest assured we would get a present later in the year. Which we always did, it might even be in the summer holidays but we still got it, and that was the nice thing about it – that they could find this way round the poverty.

In time, as more affluence and a greater commercialization of Christmas enabled Santa Claus to satisfy many more children, his significance as a symbolic figure changed. More and more parents went to great lengths to prove to their children that he had visited their home on Christmas Eve. It is odd that he should make so many personal appearances, for in the legend he is supposed to come and go in the night without being seen. There are countless family variations of the ritual whereby he leaves evidence of his visit other than presents. Joan Pringle remembers how it was in her family in Alnwick, Northumberland, between the wars:

It took a while for old Father Christmas to be transformed into a standard Santa Claus – this Northumberland Santa, complete with clogs, was pictured in 1913

Every Christmas Eve we would hang up our stockings over a large fire in the kitchen, and then mummy would place a chair for Father Christmas to sit on, because he had worked hard. Then we'd put out a plate with a mince pie, and a piece of Christmas cake, and a glass of wine for his refreshment. In the morning, there would be a few crumbs left on the plate, and a big black thumb mark, so we knew Santa Claus had been.

In Joan Pringle's family there was a good deal of dressing up as Father Christmas – there was even a Daddy Christmas played by her father for friends at an evening party – as well as the pretence that he had come and gone without being seen. The puzzle is why it was that from the 1880s onwards such pains were taken by parents to sustain their children's belief in this mysterious gift bringer. It was in this period that the old Father Christmas was superseded by Santa. In fact, there is a reference to a Dr Barnardo children's party in 1886 in which

Above: Santa as salesman, in this case for the London Co-operative Society in the 1930s

Opposite: The Santa Claus legend became almost universal between the wars, with many family variations on the theme

Overleaf: The habit of dressing up as Santa Claus caught on quickly as he came to represent charitable giving

both Father Christmas (old style) and Santa, giving out presents, appeared together. From that time on, old Father Christmas seems to disappear, to be replaced completely by the American Santa.

Ever since the 1860s when American artists remodelled the various forms of Santa Claus into a fairly consistent robust, red-robed, white-bearded figure with a sack, reindeer, and sleigh, there have been attempts to explain and understand the figure's power and appeal. Frequently, the churches have complained that at Christmastime he is far more significant for children than Jesus, and for them his popularity represents a corruption of Christmas by pagan sentiment.

The adoption of Santa Claus as a kind of ubiquitous sandwich-board man by commercial interests, such as Coca-Cola which made great play with him at Christmastime in the 1930s, has caused further concern about his significance. In France, in the 1950s, the effigy of Santa Claus was burned by clergymen who felt he was a satanic figure.

A trip to the home of Santa Claus depicted in magic lantern slides of the 1890s. The little boy's eyes almost pop out of his head as he chooses between lead soldiers and ornamental birds on perches

Claude Lévi-Strauss has pointed out Santa's connection with the Lord of Misrule of pagan winter festivals – the character elected to oversee the excesses and licence of this topsy-turvy season.

The commercial exploitation of Father Christmas can be seen as a later reassertion of the old, pre-Santa character in England – someone who was not associated with children, so much as the spirit of the season as a whole. When television advertising began in the 1950s, Father Christmas even popped up selling soap powders. Because the modern Santa Claus is essentially American in origin and concept, he has become associated with a kind of economic and cultural imperialism – a folklore export, along with jazz, Hollywood, Coca-Cola, and other Americanisms.

For the most part, however, Father Christmas, or Santa Claus – now completely interchangeable names for the same imaginary being – is simply accepted as part of our Christmas tradition. Since his arrival in the Victorian period, the greatest change in his social significance has probably been that he has become less a figure adopted by charitable ladies and more an egalitarian figure in the affluent society. But above all he was associated with the giving of gifts to children – a social custom which more than any other characterizes the modern festival.

Wrapping it up for Children

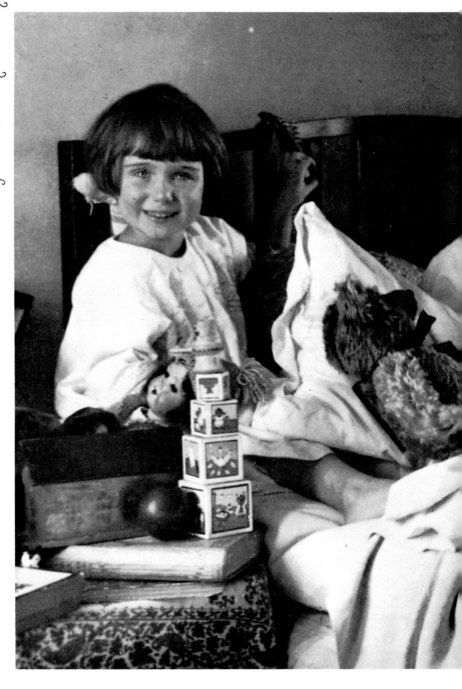

CHAPTER EIGHT

In 1850 a series of vivid descriptions of children's toys and the poor toy-maker who fashioned them, written by the social investigator Henry Mayhew, appeared in *The Morning Chronicle*. Toy-making was then a small cottage industry, and Mayhew estimated that it employed just 1,866 people in the whole of Britain, most of them working for themselves at home with their families. In Berkshire, Buckinghamshire, Wiltshire, and Glamorgan there was only one toy-maker or dealer in the whole of the county. Mayhew calculated that the amount spent on toys each year by the average child or young person under twenty was only fourpence halfpenny – a little over 1p in today's terms. This was, of course, nowhere near as paltry a sum as it might sound. Most cheap toys in those days were priced at one old penny, and for this a child could choose between a money box, a skipping rope, a box of marbles, a doll, a carved monkey that climbed a pole, a mousetrap (popular in those days as toys), and a hundred other playthings. Nevertheless, it is clear from Mayhew's evidence that toys, even of the cheapest type, were rarely bought for children in early Victorian times. Most significantly, Mayhew makes no mention of toys being given to children as Christmas presents. Today's custom of families buying sackloads of presents for their children on Christmas Day simply did not exist then, and neither did a mass production toy industry geared to supplying this market.

If presents were exchanged at this time of year, it was most likely to be on New Year's Day, a tradition in Britain and many European countries since Roman times. The presents themselves were more likely to be for adults than for children. Dickens provides a graphic description of this tradition in *The Chimes*, written in 1844:

> The streets were full of motion, and the shops were decked out gaily. The New Year, like an infant Heir to the whole world, was waited for, with welcomes, presents and rejoicings. There were books and toys for the New Year, dresses for the New Year, schemes of fortune for the New Year; new inventions to beguile it. Its life was parcelled out in almanacks . . . the coming of its moons, and stars, and tides, was known beforehand to the moment.

Previous pages: A middle-class Christmas, 1920s style. One of the most important rituals in the new child-centred Christmas was the opening of the presents

The switch from New Year's Day to Christmas Day as the time to give presents seems to have occurred for a number of reasons. From the 1840s onwards, there was an ever-increasing emphasis by the church – picked up by the popular press – on Christmas Day as 'the' celebration of the birthday of Jesus. The giving of presents on birthdays as well established by this time amongst the better off, and it was a short step from there to presents being given on Christ's birthday.

There was an old pre-Cromwellian tradition of giving sweets and small presents to children on Christmas Day which almost died out after the banning of Christmas between 1644 and 1660. By the mid nineteenth century, however, this custom was enjoying a revival, partly because of the many articles that were written in early Christmas issues of magazines on the old traditions of Christmas. Also, the increasingly child-centred emphasis of Victorian society lent itself to the development of an old tradition of giving to children.

The importing of the German tradition of the Christmas tree, which was closely associated with present giving, gave a further impetus to the giving of presents at Christmas – late on Christmas Eve. Santa Claus, arriving in Britain in the 1870s and 1880s, also added great weight to the new tradition of giving presents on Christmas Day.

However, the custom of exchanging presents on New Year's Day did not suddenly die out – it lingered on for more than twenty years. In January 1883, for example, *Tit Bits* reported:

> The New Year gifts common among equals – in the old times as now – were clothing of rich and varied descriptions, silk stockings, looking glasses, fans, caskets studded with jewels, boxes of sweetmeats, books and costly trinkets. The keeping of New Year's Day as a festival in England has nearly fallen in disuse, but the good old custom of exchanging presents of books and trinkets is still continued.

At this time it is not uncommon to find advice on present giving in magazine articles published between Christmas Day and New Year's Day; as late as 1906 a *Woman's World* editorial on what presents to give appeared on 29 December. What happened was that by the 1880s giving within the family had become well established on Christmas Day. After this it was mostly good luck charms, chains, pendants, and calendars that were given between friends on New Year's Day. One important exception is of course Scotland, where present giving on New Year's Day remained important in some rural areas until the 1950s, it died out even later among island communities on the Shetlands and Orkneys. However, in most parts of Britain, the grow-

An Edwardian street scene in the North East of England. Most toys for poorer children were made at home in the weeks before Christmas

ing emphasis on Christmas as a children's festival, which became increasingly important towards the end of the nineteenth century, finally fixed present giving on Christmas Day.

Why was there this shift towards giving presents to children at Christmastime? Most writers point to closer and more caring relationships between parents and children in Victorian times; a growing desire to keep children as children and protect them from the harshness of the real world; and the great increase in the numbers and wealth of the middle classes which gave them much more spending power in the toy shops generally. There is no doubt much truth in all these points. But too simple an acceptance of this argument often results in a 'golden age' view of old Christmases, looked back to with fond nostalgia by people who collect the antique rocking horses, clockwork trains and dolls' houses which once filled Victorian and Edwardian nurseries.

There is another, forgotten, side to the origins of this benevolence towards middle-class children at Christmas. Studies by anthropologists of the ritualistic present giving of different tribes and islanders should alert us to the fact that the giving is an exchange, the aim of which is to create or sustain a social relationship. The point is that people often give each other presents to make them feel indebted or obliged towards them, to alleviate tension or guilt, to exercise some sort of control, and to express their own social positions. If we apply this perspective to present giving in the last century then a whole new world of explanation opens up.

Victorian and Edwardian middle-class parents often had a distant relationship with their children: the 'little ones' spent much time in nurseries under the supervision of nannies, and then were quickly packed off to 'prep' and public schools, often only to be seen during the school holidays. The pressure on children to 'get on' was greater than ever before, due to the development of a much more competitive and exam-oriented society. And the Evangelical moral code of the day placed a strong emphasis on discipline, self-denial, and regimentation, which must have resulted in considerable repression of children's desires. All these kinds of factors must have created much guilt, anxiety, tension, and unhappiness, and it is not too fanciful to see Christmas in some middle-class families as a great catharsis of all these buried emotions. Christmas presents were a statement of parental love and affirmation of a caring relationship between parents and children, even though they might not see much of each other. On a more mundane level, Christmas was the time when parents rewarded their children, for 'good' behaviour during the year, with the presents they wanted.

There was, in fact, probably quite a close connection between the boom in Christmas presents for middle-class children in the second half of the nineteenth century, and the rapid development of the nursery during the same period. The home nursery quickly became the institution of Victorian and Edwardian middle-class life; to possess a nursemaid became one of the characteristics of having arrived as a member of the middle class. Mothers were often too busy with socializing, charity work, or having babies (large families with six or seven children were common in the early Victorian years) – to devote much time to the upbringing of their children. The nursery routine was partly taken up with the instruction of children in the 3 R's, but the nursery staff and governess – if there was one – needed toys and games to fill the long days. This growing demand for 'trivial nursery pursuits' gave a huge impetus to the Christmas present custom, and to the Christmas present industry, because it was precisely in the midwinter months when the children were confined to the house for long periods that the need for indoor games was greatest.

The demand was met by the development, for the first time, of an industry geared to the needs and wants of children – almost exclusively middle-class children. There were children's card games like 'Happy Families', first introduced in the 1860s; there were boxes of bricks and jigsaws and Noah's Arks; there was a whole range of board games, like 'Spoof' brought out by Chad Valley in the 1880s and 1890s; and there was a flowering of books and magazines written for slightly older children, some of the most popular of which were the *Girl's Own* and *Boy's Own Annuals*. Middle-class parents bought most of their toys, especially costly toys, at Christmas time, partly to restock the nursery for the winter months. Budding department stores like Harrods, Selfridges and Whiteleys all cashed in on this boom. The demand was such that it helped create a new breed of giant toy emporium, the most famous of which were Hamleys (then located in Oxford Street), and Gamages in Holborn, London.

The Christmas toy trade played a major role in pushing back the Christmas shopping season. In the 1880s it was unusual for Christmas presents to be advertised in the press before mid December, but by the late 1890s fashionable magazines like *The Lady* were beginning to run articles on Christmas shopping, focusing especially on children's books and toys, in late November. Trade journals show that by the 1900s the toy industry was preparing for Christmas in the previous spring and summer. The beginning of the Christmas season was marked out for many middle-class children by the postman's delivery of Gamages Christmas catalogue, which sometimes arrived as early as October. Much of Gamages business was mail order and its Christmas catalogue was an encyclopaedia – usually about 300 pages long – of every conceivable toy, puzzle, and plaything – all of which could be ordered through the post. The most popular boys' toy in the Edwardian era was the toy soldier. The front page of the 1906 catalogue warned the reader: 'We hold a stock of 500,000 soldiers of all battalions but owing to the exceptional demand at Christmastime, customers are urged to give their orders as early as possible to prevent any possibility of delay.'

Right: A parcel delivery at Southam, Gloucestershire, 1932. Overleaf: Loaded up after an inter-war Christmas shopping expedition in the West End of London. Inset: Christmas presents for adults also became big business from the late nineteenth century onwards

John Scupham, the son of a country builder, brought up in Market Rasen, Lincolnshire, in the 1900s remembers the excitement of choosing from this great catalogue in the run up to Christmas:

Christmastime alone was the time when we received new toys of any consequence. It was heralded for all of us – two boys and two girls – by the eagerly awaited plop through the letter box of Gamages inexhaustible mail order catalogue. I suppose it must have arrived about three months before Christmas itself. When I was old enough to pore over it for myself it conjured up romantic visions of huge model yachts, train sets that would fill our biggest room, and resplendent regiments equipped with canon which could fire rubber shells, and not mere matchsticks, like mine. There were real treasures in there that went far beyond those in the local toy shop, Fieldhouses. I generally got what I wanted for Christmas; I had about two or three pounds to spend on things in the catalogue, and the order would go in around late November.

The annual stampede for children's Christmas presents was fuelled even more by the promotion of 'craze toys' designed to capture the Christmas market. In 1885 Hinde's, a toy shop in London, were buying big illustrated newspaper advertisements in the run-up to Christmas to promote a doll they called 'Miss Dollie Daisie Dimple' who was billed as 'the craze of the season'. She came dressed in her best walking costume, with her travelling trunk full of fine clothes, together with 'a little book all about Miss Dimple's birthday and early history', for 'only one shilling'. For Christmas 1900, Hamleys came up with a much more original idea by introducing 'ping pong' to the dining rooms of Britain. In December 1900 *The Lady* described this 'new and popular game' which at this time was exclusive to Hamleys: 'It is most amusing and can be played on an ordinary dining room table; it is like lawn tennis, only battledores and celluloid balls are used instead of rackets; complete sets with full directions for the game can be had for 5s.6d. to 12s.6d.'

The Christmas present trade was fashioned by and for a middle-class market to such an extent that practically no attention was paid to working-class children. Woolworth's, who opened their first store in 1907, were the first to enter the working-class Christmas market on a mass scale: their cheap toys and games, which sold for a few pennies, quickly became a popular source of Christmas presents for working-class families. However, until then most poorer people usually bought their children's presents from penny bazaars, or from the trays and barrows of street traders who congregated in town and city centres in the week or two before Christmas. In London, hundreds lined the pavements of Holborn, some of them outside Gamages, where they were probably likely to pick up some extra better-off customers buying cheap novelties for their children.

The kinds of things they were selling – mostly priced at a penny – were comprehensively described in an article on street toys which appeared in the *Strand Magazine* in December 1895: there was 'the smallest bible in the world', which measured just over 2 inches long by an inch and a half wide, and which at the end contained bizarre facts about the Bible, for example, that the word Lord 'occurs 46,227 times'. There was the Dancing Yankee: 'This ingenious little toy is made of tin. By placing the thumb and second finger on his ears, and by pressing down the top of his hat with the index finger, he shoots out his tongue in scorn, rolls his eyes and moves his arms and legs as though afflicted with St Vitus's Dance.' In addition there were dancing monkeys, cock-a-doodle-do trumpets, squeaking frogs, miniature death's head coffins, and all sorts of puzzles and practical jokes.

Whatever the ingenuity of these penny toys they were rather shoddy and unappealing compared to the array of expensive playthings which filled the windows of toy shops and stores like Hamley's every Christmas. One effect of the development of the Christmas present and toy trade was to highlight the enormous gap between middle-class children and the children of the poor. Although Christmas was a festival which celebrated benevolence and good will to all, it introduced children at a very young age to the injustices and inequalities of the world. Our interviews suggest that many poorer children felt a little resentful that the toys of their dreams always ended up in the homes of better off boys and girls. But what these children lacked in toys, they often more than made up for in resourcefulness and independence, qualities which helped to compensate for the frugality of their family Christmases. Ted Harrison remembers:

I used to go off Christmas morning to the homes of the boys in posher streets near us, cos I very rarely had any proper presents for Christmas, so I thought 'I'll play with their toys', and that's what I did. We never had many toys for Christmas; we might have a lead canon or something like that. There was a shop in Oxford Street and they used to sell a bag of broken lead toys. Wonder us kids wasn't poisoned by the lead toys we had! We had lead whistles and Christ knows what, and mother used to buy us penny bags of broken toys, because she never had much. And we used to try and mend 'em. We got more enjoyment out of trying to mend these bleedin' toys than if we'd had new ones really.

Although the late Victorian and Edwardian years saw a boom in the toy trade in Britain, it was dominated by German companies, which by the eve of the First World War were manufacturing more than three-quarters of the toys sold here. This ascendancy was achieved because of cheaper prices, which in turn were made possible by the use of lowly paid outworkers. The British toy industry was in its infancy. Two of the very few toy factories were in Liverpool, where Frank Hornby oversaw the production of Meccano sets which he had invented in 1901, and in Walthamstow, East London, where Britons turned out 30 million hollow-cast toy soldiers every year. All this was to change during the Great War when German imports ended, and the government encouraged a home-grown toy industry, one of the aims of which was to keep up the morale of British families at Christmas. By 1918 this industry was employing around 100,000, many of them disabled or war veterans.

When import restrictions were lifted after the war, many small toy companies went to the wall in the face of fierce foreign competition, but the more successful grew into giant companies, one of the largest of which was Lines Brothers. In 1925 they built what was then the largest toy factory in the world in Merton, South London, to mass produce Tri-ang toys. Frank Hornby's toy empire, however, maintained its position as the brand leader for boys' presents. In 1920 he launched Hornby train sets, which along with Meccano and 'Dinky' toys (miniature cars and lorries), which he introduced in the 1930s, dominated the toy market. The fortune of this growing toy economy was closely bound up with the custom of present giving. It prospered during the inter-war years, partly because improvements in the standard of living and the general reduction of family size meant that middle-class parents – and better off working-class ones – had more money to spend on expensive presents for their children. Big presents continued to be given generally at Christmastime, with smaller ones for birthdays. John Kitchen, the son of a bank manager in East Retford, Nottinghamshire, recalls the excitement of receiving the classic boy's Christmas present of the inter-war period – the Hornby train set:

It was Christmas in 1926; I was just four and a half years old. Grandfather at that time was the general manager of the local

The inter-war years were the heyday of the train set: it became the most popular Christmas present for boys. John Kitchen (see text) was given the LNER Pullman set made by Hornby (below) for Christmas in 1925

HORNBY CLOCK WORK TRAINS
BRITISH AND GUARANTEED

This set is identical in every way with the No. 2 Pullman, L.M.S., illustrated and described on pages 23-24, except that in this case the lettering and colouring are representative of the London and North Eastern Locos and rolling-stock. The No. 2 Hornby Loco may be both braked and reversed from the track.

HORNBY No. 2 PULLMAN SET, L.N.E.R.

Hornby No. 2 Pullman Set, L.N.E.R., complete, well boxed, Price 60/-

The contents of this set are the same as those of the L.M.S. and L.N.E.R. sets. The only difference is that the components are coloured and lettered to represent G.W. Locos and rolling stock.

HORNBY No. 2 PULLMAN SET, G.W.

Hornby No. 2 Loco ... Hornby No. 2 Pullman Set, G.W., complete, well boxed, Price 60/-
Hornby Pullman Car ... ... Price 22 6 Hornby No. 2 Loco fitted for Hornby Control ... Price 25 -
... ... " 15 - Hornby No. 2 Tender ... ... " 3 6
The No. 2 Pullman Sets are also available fitted for Hornby Control, Price 65/-. Hornby Wagon ... ... " Price 2 6 (See announcement on pages 23-24).

co-operative society and they were Meccano dealers, and I well remember during the run up to Christmas of that year, going down to the shop, and seeing Hornby trains running in the window. There was a special display of trains and, of course, Meccano itself. Now Hornby trains and Meccano products in those days were 'the' Christmas presents, and if you got a train for Christmas or a Meccano set for Christmas you really had arrived. You can imagine on that Christmas morning coming downstairs in my dressing gown and seeing on the floor a circle of track, two coaches, and the engine ready to run. It was a feeling which has never in fact left me from that day to this, and the thrill of it I can still feel inside me. The train set cost 60 shillings – three pounds in modern money – a tremendous amount of money in those days because it represented at least two weeks' wages and few boys had the fortune to own a train set of this kind and of that quality.

Hornby produced cheaper train sets priced at seven shillings and sixpence in the 1920s, and Woolworths sold ones that were cheaper still, but even these were often beyond the means of many working-class families. Most of a worker's weekly wage was taken up with rent, food, and fuel bills. Also, mass unemployment and the Mean's Test effectively meant that no costly Christmas presents could be bought by the million or two families on the dole in the depression years. If any big presents were bought by poor families they were generally practical items, like children's shoes or clothing. In homes where hand-me-downs were the norm, these presents were sometimes as enthusiastically received as any expensive doll or train set. Lil Hemmings was brought up in a single-parent family in Bristol after the First World War. Her mother was a cleaner:

Christmas was the only time of the year I ever got a new dress. Most of the time it was just jumble sale stuff; shoes were second hand; mum even used to cut up her old flannelette nightdress to make petticoats. I remember when I was eight, mum used to pay sixpence every so often to a dressmaker, and she made me a velvet dress for Christmas. I can see it now with its little lace collar, and it was laid over the back of a chair on Christmas morning. I thought it was marvellous! I wore it Christmas Day and Boxing Day, then it was put away for best – Sunday best – because you didn't want to wear it out too quick.

In depressed areas like South Wales and the North East, the poor and the unemployed helped themselves by making their own Christ-

Unemployed miners in South Wales make Christmas presents for local children during the Depression years

mas presents. This age-old custom, which had provided generations of poor children with an occasional makeshift present, was very important in the Durham mining village of Byers Green in the 1920s, as Alf Todd remembers:

A monkey on a stick, that's the sort of thing we used to make for the children in days gone by, and that's what I'd got for Christmas myself when I was a child. In those days money wasn't very plentiful and most toys were made by the parents, and if not by the local joiner or blacksmith. The blacksmiths used to make your bowler hoops, which were the big thing, and the joiner would make little trolleys, little wooden houses, little barrows, and even little cots for the girls. They were homemade toys because you couldn't afford to buy toys. Just the richer people got toys, not the poor people, you ought to understand.

The growing commercialization of Christmas. In the 1950s ready-filled Christmas stockings, stuffed with small toys and chocolates, started to replace the old home-made variety filled more modestly with fruit and nuts

During the Second World War DIY toy-making for Christmas presents became a mass phenomenon, no longer restricted to poorer areas. Rationing, and the recruitment of toy factories into munitions production, meant that toys were scarce, and even middle-class parents found great difficulty in getting the Christmas presents they wanted for their children. This lack was seen to be a threat to morale on the home front: to counter it many families – encouraged by articles in women's magazines – turned their hands to toy-making. Making presents out of old scraps of wood and cardboard became a favourite pastime in air-raid shelters, wardens' posts, WVS meetings, and schools in the weeks before Christmas. And another working-class tradition – that of the hand-me-down toy – also became a popular fashion, out of necessity. The 'For Sale' and 'Wanted' columns of newspapers became packed with advertisements for second-hand toys in December.

Some children, who because their parents were poor had rarely enjoyed Christmas presents, actually fared better in the war years because of hand-outs from numerous charitable organizations dedicated to giving them a decent Christmas. The children who, at least on the surface, benefitted most were those who were evacuated from the inner-city ghettos to the homes of benevolent middle-class families, amongst whom present giving at Christmas was well established. The giving of expensive presents though sometimes seems to have created tensions between the evacuees and their own families back home, who interpreted this as the 'foster parents' trying to buy the affection of their children with luxuries they personally could not afford. In 1939 Ivy King was evacuated to Abbot's Langley in Hertfordshire from a run-down mews in Swiss Cottage, North London, where she lived with her mother – a cleaner and single parent – and her two brothers and sisters:

Before the war we didn't celebrate Christmas very much really because we were what was classed as a poor family in those days. We only had a stocking with a few sweets, fruit, and a very small toy. But when I was evacuated it was entirely different, because I went to a middle-aged couple who had no children and they idolized me. I was the 'pretty little girl with the black ringlets', because I was only seven at the time. My first Christmas I remember very well. They said, 'Go in the front room and there'll be a surprise for you under the armchair.' And when I looked there was this big white box with this beautiful doll in it. It was a china doll and I don't remember having a doll before that in my life. And we had a Christmas tree and Christmas crackers – things like that which I'd never had at home; I really thought I was in wonderland! It wasn't till after the war I remembered how much I had hurt my mother because every time she came to see me she asked if I wanted to go home with her and every time I said no. Eventually I went back in 1944, but unfortunately the harm was done between mother and me, and we were never really close again. In my heart I don't think she ever forgave me for it.

Most working-class families had to wait until the 'never-had-it-so-good' years of the late 1950s before they were able to indulge their children with 'big' Christmas presents. The familiar story of full employment, higher wages, and the end of austerity, at last brought Hornby Dublo train sets and expensive dolls within the grasp of the majority of the population. Charles McEwan, who, as we saw in Chapter One, for a combination of religious and economic reasons had not been able to celebrate Christmas properly during his Edinburgh childhood, was determined to make the most of the festive present giving with his own children in the 1950s:

My wife Betty and I used to go overboard at Christmastime on the toys. There would be soldiers by the hundred, cowboy's outfits, nurse's outfits, and later on Scalextric. There'd be so many toys we'd hide them behind the sideboard, and we'd have to move it out from the wall so that there was enough room to put them behind it. And we had a special Christmas Day ritual. We'd get up early at about six o'clock in the morning and take the presents in and put them round the tree. Then we'd light the fire and put a record on the record player – a Christmas song, Bing Crosby's 'White Christmas' was the favourite. Then we'd come out and lock the door and the children were only allowed in when they'd dressed up in their Sunday best, their best trousers and everything, out of respect for Christmas. I think we were sort of compensating for our own childhood when our parents couldn't really afford proper Christmas presents for us, because Christmas now was the highlight of our year. The kids would come up to us and say, 'This is the best Christmas we've ever had', and that would make it all worthwhile.

But there was to be a sting in the tail of this massive growth in Christmas present giving among all classes in the post-war years. Children's Christmas toys had become very big business and from the 1970s onward American multi-national companies like Fisher-Price, Mattel, and Hasbro moved in to corner the market. Their success was

From the mid 1950s onwards the Christmas toy industry boomed, fuelled by rising wages and an increasingly affluent society

largely due to the use of cheap labour in the Far East and heavy TV advertising of new 'craze toys' like Star Wars puppets, Masters of the Universe, and Transformers in the weeks before Christmas. The British toy industry, which had provided thousands of jobs, was virtually killed off, and famous names like Meccano ceased production. The toy trade had turned full circle, being dependent again upon foreign imports just as it had in the 1880s. But the use of television to promote mass toy sales highlights one major change. Now, the toy manufacturers appeal to working-class children and their parents to sell many of their toys at Christmas. A custom which began in the exclusive atmosphere of the nursery triumphed in the slick world of mass television advertising.

Epilogue

In the post-war world many people complain that the Christmas festival has lost its meaning as a social ritual. There are two fairly obvious explanations for the belief that Christmas has been stripped of much of its significance and character in our more affluent age. Firstly, adults, recalling their childish thrill of Christmas, always imagine that the magic has been lost. As a rule, their children do not agree. Secondly, there is now such a high consumption throughout the year of food and consumer goods that the significance of an annual feast and present giving has clearly been diminished. Affluence takes the spice out of a great many experiences, and no doubt some of the former poignancy of Christmas has gone.

On the other hand, there is no doubt that it was only in an age of affluence that the Dickensian ideal of everyone being able to celebrate Christmas more or less like the middle classes became a possibility. In this sense, Christmas as a festival has triumphed, even if it appears to have lost some of its social significance as it has done so.

Nevertheless, it remains the single most important annual festival in Britain today, and still exerts a tremendous power over everybody. Roads and trains are crammed with people going home to their families. Being on your own at Christmas is regarded as a kind of tragedy, and for the large number of people who have no family – or no family that they want to be with – it can be one of the most miserable times of the year. It is quite possible this will change with time: that gradually, as with the adoption of new rituals in the nineteenth century, in the late twentieth century some other season will be revived and will rival Christmas, as the Whitsun holidays once did in country areas not so long ago. From the time it first arose, the Christmas festival has been evolving. It is only very recently it has been enjoyed to the full by the mass of the population. It is surely this fact, and not the imagined loss of its significance, which is the most remarkable feature of the festival.

Index